Ontology and Ethics in Sartre's Early Philosophy

Ontology and Ethics in Sartre's Early Philosophy

Yiwei Zheng

LEXINGTON BOOKS

A Division of
ROWMAN & LITTLEFIELD PUBLISHERS, INC.
Lanham • Boulder • New York • Toronto • Oxford

LEXINGTON BOOKS

A division of Rowman & Littlefield Publishers, Inc.
A wholly owned subsidary of The Rowman & Littlefield Publishing Group, Inc.
4501 Forbes Boulevard, Suite 200
Lanham, MD 20706

PO Box 317
Oxford
OX2 9RU, UK

British Library Cataloguing in Publication Information Available

Library of Congress Cataloging-in-Publication Data

Zheng, Yiwei, 1972-
  Ontology and Ethics in Sartre's Early Philosophy / Yiwei Zheng.
    p. cm.
  Includes bibliographical references and index.
  ISBN 0-7391-1117-5 (alk. paper)
    1. Sartre, Jean Paul, 1905—Ethics. 2. Sartre, Jean Paul, 1905—Ontology. I. Title.
B317.J64 2005
183'.2—dc22   2005004313

Printed in the United States of America

♾™ The paper used in this publication meets the minimum requirements of American
National Standard for Information Sciences—Permanence of Paper for Printed Library
Materials, ANSI/NISO Z39.48–1992.

To

Paul Vincent Spade

with admiration

Contents

Abbreviations of Frequently Cited
Works of Jean-Paul Sartre

BN	*Being and Nothingness: A Phenomenological Essay on Ontology*
EN	*L'Etre et le néant: Essai d'ontologie phénoménologique*
NE	*Notebooks for an Ethics*
PI	*The Psychology of Imagination*
TE	*The Transcendence of the Ego: An Existentialist Theory of Consciousness*
TL	*La Transcendence de l'ego: Esquisse d'une description phénoménologique*

Full information on these works is given in the bibliography.

Acknowledgments

This work develops from the doctoral dissertation I wrote at Indiana University, Bloomington. I owe thanks to many who assisted me during my graduate studies: in particular, to Paul Eisenberg, Paul Franks, David McCarty, and Paul Spade for serving on my dissertation committee and for commenting on varius drafts of the dissertation, to Hans Kim, Ming Xu, Xiaomei Yang, John Ceballes, Michael Dunn, Brian McDonald, and Rondo Keele for many stimulating and enjoyable conversions, and to Ronald Bruzina, Jane McIntyre, Nicholas Moutafakis, and Thomas Olshewsky for encouraging me to continue graduate studies in philosophy.

Parts of the work were presented and published at various forums. Many people have provided me with useful feedback. My thanks go to Sven Arvidson, Joseph Bien, Linda Bell, Joseph Catalano, David Detmer, Peter Hutcheson, Mark Maller, William McBride, Frederick Neuhouser, Joseph Walsh, and Kathleen Wider for their valuable comments and friendly criticisms. I have benefitted from the correspondence with Rocco Gennaro, James Rose, David Weberman, and Zhenming Zhai. My colleagues at St. Cloud, including Myron Anderson, John Bahde, Kathleen Gill, Carla Johnson, Xiusheng Liu, Matthias Steup, and Casey Swank, gave me various sorts of help. I am especially grateful to Steven Hendley, who read the entire manuscript and gave me many helpful comments.

Above all, I would like to thank Paul Spade, who not only stimulated my interest in Sartre and directed my dissertation, but also serves as my model of an exemplary scholar and teacher. This work is dedicated to him.

Parts of several chapters were published in varius journals. I am grateful to *Sartre Studies International, Southern Journal of Philosophy, Southwest Philosophy Review* for their permission to use the previously published articles.

Finally, I would like to express my gratitude to my parents, Minxiang Zheng and Yaqin Wo, for their love and support.

Introduction

Taken separately and independently, Jean-Paul Sartre's early ethical and ontological theories are fairly well studied and understood. Nevertheless, at the end of *Being and Nothingness* Sartre made the curious claim that his ethical views, not only in broad outline but also in detail, follow from his ontology and are based on it. Scholars are divided in their reactions to this claim. Some seem to accept it, but they don't bother or take little trouble to work out the passage from ontology to ethics. Others reject or ignore the claim, treating Sartre's ethics as an independent view in its own right, without worrying too much about what it is supposed to be based on.

How exactly should we understand Sartre's curious claim? To some critics this claim can be dismissed at the outset. Their reason is as follows: What did Sartre mean by claiming that his ethics follows from and is based on his ontology? The phrase 'Sartre's ethics following from his ontology' seems to suggest that Sartre's ontological theses constitute a *sufficient* condition for his ethical doctrines. The phrase 'Sartre's ethics being based on his ontology' seems to suggest that Sartre's ontological theses constitute a *necessary* condition for his ethical doctrines. However, on the one hand, it is too strong to claim that Sartre's ontology is sufficient for his ethics. We know that there is an is/ought distinction, and there is no way that we can deduce ethical statements from ontological statements. On the other hand, it is too weak to claim that Sartre's ontology is necessary for his ethics. If Sartre's aim had been just to show that his ontology is needed for his ethics, he would not have struggled so hard in *Notebooks for an Ethics* to find out a passage from ontology to ethics.

I agree with the critics that, by claiming his ethics follows from and is based on his ontology, Sartre did not just mean that his ontology is necessary for his ethics. But I disagree that ontology being sufficient for ethics or ontology being necessary for ethics exhausts the possible interpretations of Sartre's claim.

I think that by claiming his ethics follows from and is based on his ontology, Sartre did mean a sort of logical connection between his ontology and ethics. But the connection is *not* a *context-free*, strictly logical implication, as the critics suggest. Sartre's claim should not be understood as that the ontological theses implies the ethical doctrines *without any context*, i.e., the ontological theses are the *only* proper axioms used in derivation. Rather, it should be understood that the ontology implies the ethics *in the context where we use our ordinary understanding of and assumptions about the connections between the ontological and ethical concepts as additional proper axioms in derivation.* In other words, the concern Sartre had with respect to the relation between his ontology and ethics is this: Given our ordinary understanding of and assumptions about the connections between the fundamental ontological and ethical concepts, what ethical theory would be *prima facie* plausible if we adopt the ontology developed in *Being and Nothingness* rather than the naive ontology in ordinary life? Understood in this way, the passage from ontology to ethics seems to be both *possible* and *non-trivial*. For example, if we have an ontological thesis saying that we are absolutely free in doing X, it is *prima facie* plausible that we have an ethical doctrine saying that we are absolutely responsible for doing X and for the results of doing X.

In the work that follows, I aim to answer the question whether Sartre's early ethics follows from his ontology. I study carefully the important notions in Sartre's early ontology and ethics, including some notoriously difficult ones. Using these studies as the basis, I examine in detail how Sartre's early ethics is supposed to based on his ontology in *Being and Nothingness*. My conclusion is that, although there are more connections between Sartre's ontology and his ethics than is typically recognized, Sartre's claim is nonetheless false—there are unbridgeable gaps between his ontology and ethics that cannot be filled in.

I organize this work in the following way:

The first two chapters are preparatory. In chapter 1, I clarify some important technical terms in Sartre's early philosophy. Among others, I offer a "present-tense-feel" account of Sartre's non-positional consciousness. In chapter 2, I investigate the general feature of Sartre's ontological project in *Being and Nothingness* through a comparison between Sartre's and Husserl's theories of intentionality.

In the ensuing three chapters I examine in turn three key notions in Sartre's early ontology, "freedom," "bad faith," and "pure reflection." In chapter 3, I study the ontological characters of freedom in *Being and Nothingness*. By distinguishing two parts of non-positional consciousness (of) freedom, I argue that Sartre's claim that freedom is absolute is compatible with his claim that freedom is limited. In chapter 4, I study the ontological characteristics of bad faith that Sartre presented in *Being and Nothingness* through a detailed examination of the conditions of the possibility of bad faith. On the basis of my interpretation, I argue against Ronald Santoni's thesis that the ontological characteristics of bad faith have salient and non-trivial ethical implications. In chapter 5, I study the ontological characteristics of pure reflection in *Being and Nothingness*. I argue that a philosophical method having pure reflection as a component satisfies a basic requirement for any sound philosophical method—the requirement that a sound philosophical method must produce normative universal knowledge.

After examining three key notions in Sartre's early ontology, I proceed to develop an interpretation of Sartre's theory of authenticity. In chapter 6, I argue that in authenticity we do not reject the project of trying to be God, contrary to Thomas Anderson's claim. In chapter 7, I discuss in detail three ethical features of authenticity that Sartre presented in *Notebooks for an Ethics*.

In chapter 8, I use the results obtained in the previous chapters to explore the possible ways to ground Sartre's ethics on the basis of his ontology. I conclude that Sartre's ethical theory does not really follow from his ontology, no matter how eagerly he hoped it would.

Chapter One

Basic Terminologies

Introduction

In this chapter, I clarify some basic notions in Sartre's early philosophy. I start by discussing a mistranslation in Forrest Williams and Robert Kirkpatrick's translation of *The Transcendence of the Ego*. I then criticize Kathleen Wider's bodily account of non-positional consciousness and offer my "present-tense-feel" account. Next, I discuss the Being-in-itself from three aspects and study the meanings of "nothingness" in *The Psychology of Imagination* and in *Being and Nothingness*. Finally, I distinguish the various senses of the paradoxical doctrine that consciousness is not what it is and is what it is not.

Unreflected Consciousness and Unreflective Consciousness

Let me start with the term *conscience irréfléchie*. This term was mistranslated as 'unreflected consciousness' in Forrest Williams and Robert Kirkpatrick's translation of *The Transcendence of the Ego* (TL, 24, 29–32, 36–37, 39–44, 48, 57, 70–72; TE, 41, 45–48, 53, 55, 57–61, 65, 74, 88–91), and correctly translated as 'unreflective consciousness' in Bernard Frechtman's translation of *The Emotions: Outline of a Theory* and in Hazel Barnes' translation of *Being and Nothingness*.

The meaning of this term in *The Emotions* and in *Being and Nothingness* is quite clear: It simply refers to an unreflective consciousness, a consciousness that does not take another consciousness from the same stream as its intentional object.[1] It is synonymous with the term *conscience*

1

non-réfléchi ('non-reflective consciousness') or the term *conscience préréflexif*('pre-reflective consciousness'). Thus, Frechtman's and Barnes' translation is correct.

Nevertheless, the meaning of *conscience irréfléchie* in *The Transcendence of the Ego* is *ambiguous*. While in most cases *irréfléchie* refers to the unreflective state of consciousness, at three places it refers to the *unreflected* state of consciousness, i.e., the state of any *living* consciousness, whether the consciousness is reflective or unreflective, as long as the consciousness is not an entity posited by a reflective consciousness.

Among the thirty-four occurrences[2] of this word *irréfléchie* in the French edition of *The Transcendence of the Ego*, at thirty-one occurrences it refers to the unreflective state of consciousness. For example, when Sartre first introduced the word *irréfléchie*, he took it to designate the unreflective state of consciousness:

> We should add that this consciousness of consciousness—except in the case of reflective consciousness which we shall dwell on later—is not *positional*, which is to say that consciousness is not for itself its own object. Its object is by nature outside of it, and that is why consciousness *posits* and *grasps* the object in the same act. Consciousness knows itself only as absolute inwardness. We shall call such a consciousness: consciousness in the first degree, or *unreflected* [unreflective] consciousness [*conscience irréfléchie*]. (TL, 24; TE, 40–41)

However, at the following three occurrences of *irréfléchie* in *The Transcendence of the Ego*, it refers to the *unreflected* state of consciousness:

> All reflecting consciousness is, indeed, in itself unreflected [*irréfléchie*], and a new act of the third degree is necessary in order to posit it. (TL, 29; TE, 45)
> But is it not precisely the reflective act which gives birth to the *me* in the reflected consciousness? Thus would be explained how every thought apprehended by intuition possesses an I, without falling into the difficulties noted in the preceding section. Husserl would be the first to acknowledge that an unreflected [*irréfléchie*] thought undergoes a radical modification in becoming reflected. (TL, 29; TE, 45)
> [T]here is an unreflected [*irréfléchie*] act of reflection, without an *I*, which is directed on a reflected consciousness. (TL, 36; TE, 53)

In these three passages, *irréfléchie* was used to distinguish the living consciousness from the *posited* consciousness—consciousness posited as an intentional object of a reflective consciousness. Perhaps because they took these three passages as the samples for generalization, Williams and Kirkpatrick translated *conscience irréfléchie* as 'unreflected consciousness'. But this translation is not correct, because all other thirty-one occurrences *conscience irréfléchie* refers to the unreflective consciousness.

So far we have seen the difference between the unreflective consciousness and the unreflected consciousness. What is the relation between the unreflective consciousness and the pre-reflective *cogito*? The pre reflective *cogito* is the self-awareness (of) the unreflective consciousness, the self-awareness that Sartre called the "non-positional consciousness" (of) the unreflective consciousness. In the next section let's look closely at the side of non-positional consciousness.

Non-positional Consciousness

The notion of "non-positional consciousness" is central to Sartre's early philosophy. It is essential to his ontology, since it is in terms of non-positional consciousness that consciousness is distinguished from unconscious things on the one hand, and from "knowledge"[3] on the other. It is also essential to his ethics, since it is presupposed by "bad faith"[4] and the key stage to "authenticity"[5]—"pure reflection"[6]—involves a reflective recognition of non-positional consciousness.

"Non-positional consciousness" is also one of the most mysterious notions in Sartre's early philosophy. Although the distinction between positional and non-positional consciousness is among the first things we encounter in Sartre's early philosophy, Sartre explained little about non-positional consciousness in non-technical terms. Furthermore, in spite of its importance, non-positional consciousness is not well explained in the secondary literature: Some commentators simply quoted Sartre in explaining it[7] while some others took wild guesses.[8] In her recent book *The Bodily Nature of Consciousness*, Kathleen Wider proposed an interesting account of non-positional consciousness by appealing to the "body's self-awareness in sensorimotor activity."[9] In this section, I argue against Wider's interpretation and offer my "present-tense-feel" account of non-positional consciousness.

As early as in *The Transcendence of the Ego*, Sartre introduced the distinction between positional (or thetic) and non-positional (or non-thetic) consciousness (TL, 28–29; TE, 44–45). There and in other places he claimed that every consciousness has two sides[10]: the positional side, where consciousness is aware of an intentional transcendent object, and the non-positional side, where consciousness is aware (of) the way that it is positionally aware of the intentional object.[11] How should we understand that?

The positional consciousness is a reformulation of a common understanding of intentionality—our mental activities are always "directed upon" some objects. For Sartre "directedness" means a not necessarily verbal contact with the object, which occurs in the form of taking a position on something. For example, when I fear an approaching lion, I adopt a position of fearing on the approaching lion or the situation in which the lion emerges. When I withdraw from my fear and give an objective description of the situation as "there comes a lion," I take a linguistic-descriptive position on the lion or the situation, which appears as the intentional object of my consciousness. To capture the sense of directedness, the not necessarily verbal contact with the object, let me use the word 'acquaintance'.[12]

The non-positional consciousness is one of Sartre's greatest innovations; and, as far as I know, there is no other philosopher who has paid as much attention as Sartre to the peculiar conscious life designated by "non-positional consciousness." Sartre claimed that non-positional consciousness is the self-consciousness where consciousness is aware (of) the way it is positionally aware of the intentional object. What does it mean exactly?

According to Wider in *The Bodily Nature of Consciousness*, Sartre's non-positional consciousness is or should have been the bodily self-consciousness, i.e., the body's awareness of itself as a point of view on the world, as a center of reference and action.[13] Wider said:

> The most basic form of self-consciousness must be bodily awareness. . .
> For Sartre, the world and the body are always present to consciousness but in different ways. If I am reading, I am positionally conscious of the words on the page but against the ground of the world. The world as ground indicates my body as corporal totality. . . . Sartre uses the example of reading. In reading the eyes appear as figure on the ground of the corporal totality just as the words appear as figure on the ground of the world. So both the specific organ, the eyes in the case of reading, and the body as a totality are present to consciousness when consciousness is present to the world. My awareness of my own body "forms a part of that distance-less existence of positional consciousness for itself."[14]

There is no doubt that Wider's account of bodily self-awareness helps us better understand Sartre's discussion of the awareness of one's body as subject in *part three* of *Being and Nothingness*. Nevertheless, it is hard to maintain—in Sartre's framework—that non-positional consciousness in general is or should have been Wider's bodily self-awareness.

Non-positional consciousness cannot simply be equated with Wider's bodily self-awareness, for two reasons. First, although Sartre admitted that the bodily self-awareness—the awareness of one's body as subject—is *a part of* the structure of non-positional consciousness with respect to certain consciousnesses, he *denied* the complete and total identification of the bodily self-awareness with non-positional consciousness (as Wider recognized) (EN, 394–95; BN, 434). Second, Wider's bodily self-awareness does not seem to capture the sense of 'non-positional consciousness' in general. For it is not clear how Wider's bodily self-awareness accounts for the non-positional consciousness (of) a mental act that involves no sensory interaction with the world, e.g., the non-positional consciousness (of) adding two numbers, the non-positional consciousness (of) applying *modus ponens*, etc. In other words, although the bodily account explains *the peculiar features of a certain group of non-positional consciousnesses*—the group that involves one's awareness of body as subject—it does not seem to explain *the characteristic feature that defines all non-positional consciousness*.

Moreover, it is hard to maintain—under Sartre's system—that non-positional consciousness should have been the bodily self-awareness. First, according to Sartre, non-positional consciousness occurs in all conscious activities, insofar as all conscious activities are self-conscious, and non-positional consciousness is self-consciousness. Now if non-positional consciousness were just the bodily self-awareness, there would be no non-positional consciousness in those consciousnesses that involve no sensory interaction with the world. Consequently, we have to reject or qualify either the claim that all conscious activities are self-conscious or the claim that non-positional consciousness is self-consciousness. Second, in "the ontological proof" Sartre used non-positional consciousness to derive being-in-itself by treating non-positional consciousness as a revealing intuition (EN, 29; BN, 23). But if non-positional consciousness were just the awareness of body as subject, how would the ontological proof work in the group of consciousnesses that Sartre called "conception" in *The Psychology of Imagination* (PI, 9)? In sum, we cannot hold the thesis that non-positional consciousness should have been the bodily self-awareness without bringing significant changes to Sartre's system.

Having argued that Wider's bodily account does not capture the sense of "non-positional consciousness" in general, I now offer a "present-tense-feel" account of non-positional consciousness which I argue matches nearly[15] everything Sartre said concerning non-positional consciousness.

To start, let me use the word 'feels' to designate non-positional consciousness, since it is the best word I can find in ordinary language whose sense approximates that of "non-positional consciousness." To have an idea of what "feels" is, consider this example: Suppose I am thinking hard to construct a logical proof, and my attention is completely absorbed in the proof. Yet, even as I lose myself in the world of symbols at the moment, I am a "feel" (of) the intensity of my thought. Suppose at one stage I choose to use the inference rule *modus ponens* on two formulas. At that time I am a "feel" (of) applying the rule *modus ponens*. Suppose I suddenly see the last step of the proof. I am a "feel" (of) the abrupt and clear seeing act. Suppose I then say aloud: "Oh, great!" while seeing the last step of the proof. I am a mixture of various "feels": a "feel" that I am making a linguistic exclamation (which includes the "feel" that I will make certain sounds), a "feel" (of) the movement of my voice-producing muscle, and a "feel" (of) the fluctuation of sounds in connection with the "feel" (of) making exclamation. In general, a "feel" "pops up" whenever we have a project-related acquaintance. More precisely, a "feel" (or "feels") occurs when and only when (1) a mental act[16] is initiated and exercised, or (2) our mental life moves from one state to another in the broad sense of "state."[17]

The choice of the word 'feel' for non-positional consciousness and the example above might mislead one to think that "feels" are just qualitative states. But "feels" are different from qualitative states. First, unlike qualitative states, "feels" do not *always* have distinctive[18] qualities. Project-related "feels" such as the "feel" (of) applying *modus ponens* and the "feel" (of) opening an envelope do not have distinctive qualities,[19] and they are described and distinguished from others (linguistically) *in terms of their functional relations to the positional objects in the relevant projects.*[20] Second, unlike qualitative states, "feels" are *not* states. For we *have or undergo* states, but we *are* "feels." A "feel" is the living of an ongoing project or experience. *It is a mixture of attending-to*[21] *and the project or experience attended to.* This does not mean that attending-to and the project or experience attended to are *two sides* of the non-positional "feel," as if attending-to were "the way to feel" and the project or experience attended to were "something felt." Rather, it means that 'attending-to' and 'the project or experience attended to' are *two incomplete descriptions* of the non-positional "feel," and that the non-positional "feel" is a *single-sided being* that might be understood as *"attending-to-invested-in-the-project-or-experience."* *Here my point is that a "feel" is none of "the way to feel," "the thing felt," and "the totality of the way to feel and the thing felt."* It is not "the way to feel," because we don't have another consciousness of the project or experience felt to contrast it ("the way to feel") with. It is not "the thing felt," because we don't have another consciousness of the attending-to to contrast it ("the thing felt") with. It is not "the totality of the way to feel and the thing felt," because in it we do not have a contrast between the object of consciousness and the conscious act; rather, we have a single-sided mixture of attending-to and the project or experience attended to.

Another way to understand and characterize "feels" is to think about our first-person *present-tense reports.* In ordinary language, how do we make present-tense reports from the first-person perspective? Or to put it a different way, how, in an appropriate circumstance, do we know that we should make a present-tense report ("I am doing X") instead of a past-tense report ("I did X") or a future-tense report ("I will do X")? It must be through the witnessing[22] of a certain time-sensitive element[23] that we know we should make a present-tense report. But what exactly is this time-sensitive element? It cannot be *the observable results* of our action (e.g., the movement of a ball as a result of my kicking the ball). For at the time when the results are there, we are only able to make past-tense reports of our action (e.g., "I kicked a ball"), and at the time when the results are not there, we are only able to make future-tense reports of our action (e.g., "I will kick a ball"). It cannot be *the anticipations* we have in connection with our action (e.g., the anticipation that a ball will move in such and such away after I kick it) either. For at the time when the anticipations are fulfilled, we are only able to make past-tense reports of our action (e.g., "I kicked a ball"), and at the time when the anticipations are not fulfilled, we are only able to make future-tense reports of our action (e.g., "I will kick a ball"). What then is this time-sensitive element, the witnessing of which leads us to make a present-tense report? Well, *it is precisely a "feel" (of) X, as something we are at the moment of our doing or having X, the witnessing of which leads us to make a present-tense report, and without which we cannot have the linguistic behavior of present-tense reports.*

"Feels" are not, but have close relations, with feelings. "Feels" are not feelings, because feelings are objects posited in reflective consciousness whereas "feels" are not. And yet "feels" have close relations with feelings, because feelings are reflective hypostatizations of certain "feels," i.e., the reflectively posited objects when we think about certain "feels." For example, in a situation where I see and fear an approaching lion, the "feel" I am is my attentive living of the non-linguistic, terrified experience in the unreflective state, whereas my fear (as my feeling) is something posited when I exit the unreflective state and reflect upon the non-linguistic "feel."

To understand further the characteristics of "feels," let me contrast "feels" with acquaintances in the following three respects:

1. There is something that limits our freedom in acquaintances, while there is no such limitation in "feels." In an acquaintance, the "revealed" object is grasped as being different from and independent of our acquainting, and as, in one way or another, conditioning or limiting the freedom of our acquainting. For example, in seeing a table, I cannot alter what I see just by my whim; I don't have the freedom to make the table disappear or to turn it into a chair. However, things are different in "feels." The consciousness which I am a non-positional "feel" (of) *is* the "feel," and accordingly the "feel" is not conditioned by the consciousness which I have the "feel" (of). In this sense we say that there is no passivity in "feels."

2. Some acquaintances (e.g., linguistic descriptions) are linguistic, whereas all "feels" are non-linguistic. Although not all acquaintances are linguistic, e.g., emotional or actional consciousness, a great number of acquaintances—knowledge*—are linguistic. In contrast, none of our "feels" is linguistic, and a person is "feels" even if she does not know any language at all.[24] This character of "feels," plus the fact that our language is not designed to communicate "feels" other than the "feels" that are posited as feelings in reflection, partly explain why in many cases it is extraordinarily difficult to describe "feels."

3. Acquaintances are instantaneous, whereas "feels" are continuous. In acquaintance, the intentional object is grasped or understood as *without duration*. This does not mean that acquaintance takes no time, but that the grasped or intuited meanings in acquaintance (1) come and go in a flash and (2) are self-sufficient, with no indication within themselves of any connection with the past and future meanings. In contradistinction, "feels" are continuous; e.g., a painful "feel" is an unbroken process. This doesn't mean that my entire conscious life, from birth to death, is an unbroken process. From time to time, I certainly jump from one "feel" to another; e.g., at this moment I am a "feel" in connection with my thinking of A, at

next moment I am another "feel" in connection with my thinking of B. But I cannot be a "feel" (of) the gap among "feels"—I am always this or that particular "feel."

This "present-tense-feel" account of non-positional consciousness accommodates the following six remarks by Sartre:

1. Sartre claimed that whenever there is a (project-related) positional consciousness, there is also a non-positional consciousness. In my account this is true, because (a) whenever there is a (project-related) positional consciousness, there is a fluctuation of mental states (insofar as a mental act is initiated and exercised), and (b) we have non-positional "feels" whenever our mental states fluctuate.

2. Sartre repeatedly said that non-positional consciousness is not knowledge* (EN, 20; BN, 14). It is easy to explain this in my account, because all "feels" are non-linguistic.

3. Sartre used non-positional consciousness to characterize the being of consciousness rather than an idea of consciousness. This is true in my interpretation, because "feels" are exactly what captures our being—our living of conscious life—in the present tense.

4. Sartre took "hedonic feelings," e.g., pleasure (by "pleasure" Sartre meant the "feel" [of] pleasure, not pleasure as a reflectively posited feeling) as non-positional consciousness (EN, 21; BN, 14–15). This becomes easily understandable when we interpret non-positional consciousness as "feels."

5. Sartre said that non-positional consciousness is a flow. This makes sense under my interpretation. For "feels" are aroused when and only when there is a fluctuation of mental states, which explains the fact that non-positional consciousness is essentially a flow, a becoming.

6. Sartre said that non-positional consciousness is responsible for the unification of a theme (e.g., counting cigarettes) in a mental act (EN, 19–20; BN, 13). This is accounted for by my thesis that "feels" are continuous: When I am a certain "feel" in a mental act, the operative intention of the particular "feel" is present all along throughout the mental act.

To recapitulate, in the foregoing, I have offered a "present-tense-feel" account of non-positional consciousness, and I have argued that my account fits well with most of Sartre's remarks on non-positional consciousness. Before we move to the next topic, let me stress again that the notion of "non-positional consciousness" is crucial to Sartre's early philosophy: It is in terms of recognizing the non-positional "feels" that we can meaningfully talk about the being of consciousness (i.e., consciousness in the *unreflected* state) and that we can successfully distinguish the being of consciousness from an idea of consciousness (the posited or reflected consciousness) in (impure) reflection.

Being-In-Itself

Sartre claimed that there are two fundamental sorts of entities: Being-for-itself (or simply for-itself) and Being-in-itself (or simply in-itself). 'Being-for-itself' is Sartre's special term for consciousness, whose being is characterized by the non-positional "feel" we discussed in the previous section. In this section, I will discuss three issues concerning the being-in-itself (the being of the phenomenon): (1) the relation between the in-itself and the intentional object of the for-itself, (2) the relation between the in-itself and the phenomenon of being, and (3) the epistemological problem concerning how we can know anything about the in-itself.

Before we start the discussion of the being-in-itself, let me correct a mistranslation in Barnes' translation of *Being and Nothingness*.

In Barnes' translation of the *Introduction* to *Being and Nothingness*, the French words *dévoilement* in *section II* and *révélation* in *section V* were both translated as 'revelation' (EN, 15; BN, 8; EN, 29; BN, 23). However, in their respective context *dévoilement* and *révélation* mean different things. In *section II*, Sartre claimed that the being of the phenomenon (the being-in-itself) is *la condition de tout dévoilement* ("the condition of all revelation" in Barnes' translation) (EN, 15; BN, 8). And *in section V* Sartre claimed that the being-in-itself is *un révélé* ("something revealed" in Barnes' translation) (EN, 29; BN, 23). But the being-in-itself cannot be both the condition of all revelation and something revealed, for something revealed is a revelation, and how can something revealed be the condition of itself? Understood in their respective context, *dévoilement* characterizes the interpretation and the understanding of the being-in-itself in the positional consciousness, whereas *révélation* represents an aspect of the original ontological relation between the for-itself and the in-itself, which relation is manifested in the non-positional consciousness. Hence, *dévoilement* and *révélation* are different. Hereinafter, I shall translate *dévoilement* as 'disclosure', and *révélation* as 'revelation'. While the being-in-itself is something revealed, it is the condition of all disclosure.

This said, let me look at the relation between the being-in-itself and the intentional object. The first thing to note is that *we should not simply equate the being-in-itself with any intentional object.* For an intentional object, whether it is a physical thing, an imaginary entity, an essence, a posited consciousness, etc., has determinations of various sorts (e.g., shape, color, quality, quantity, etc.), whereas the being-in-itself has none (BN, 27, 249; EN, 32, 228–29). However, most intentional objects bear some relations to the being-in-itself.

When the intentional object is a concrete physical thing, e.g., a table, it is a disclosure, a "hypostatized nothingness" arising out of the original ontological relation[25] between the for-itself and the in-itself.[26] A physical object—as a combination of properties and qualities—neither hides nor discloses the being-in-itself, since what we grasp at the positional side of consciousness, the properties and qualities of the object, neither suggest that there is something behind them nor indicate that they belong to the in-itself (EN, 15; BN, 8). Furthermore, the in-itself is not the matter on the basis of which a physical object is made; it is not the Aristotelian matter, which is the material component of the substance. It is rather the "condition of revelation [disclosure]"[27] (EN, 15, 28-29; BN, 8, 23-24); it enables us to perceive the physical object.

When the intentional object is an imaginary entity, e.g., a unicorn, it bears a mediate relation to the in-itself. Since an imaginary entity consists of various parts that come from the actual physical objects, and since these "borrowed" parts are disclosed on the basis of the original relation between the for-itself and the in-itself, the imaginary entity bears subsequently a mediate relation to the in-itself.

For a posited consciousness, e.g., a consciousness in which one or more of the "I" or the "me," the agent's state, quality, and action is posited, it is posited as having some properties possessed by physical things (EN, 207–8; BN, 224–25)—that physical things have existence independent of my will, that physical things completely coincide with themselves—properties that are derived from two characters of the phenomenon of being, that the in-itself is in-itself, and that the in-itself is what it is (EN, 32–34; BN, 27–29). Thus, being disclosed as a for-itself-in-itself hybrid, the posited consciousness resembles the phenomenon of being-in-itself.

Next, let's discuss the relation between the in-itself and the phenomenon of being, starting from a clarification of the notions of "phenomenon" and "the phenomenon of being." In *Being and Nothingness*, phenomenon or appearance means the disclosed content of an object in perception, not the subjective experience of perceiving the object or the perceived intentional object (EN, 13–14; BN, 6–7). For example, suppose I see a cube in front of me. The phenomenon or appearance is the part of the cube that I see, not the cube itself or my experience of seeing. The phenomenon of being is a special kind of phenomenon, the phenomenon disclosed in those peculiar consciousnesses such as boredom and nausea. Let's look at it closely.

In *section II* of the *Introduction* to *Being and Nothingness*, the "phenomenon of being" was first introduced as the intentional object of boredom or nausea.[28] Immediately after that, Sartre asked the question whether the phenomenon of being thus understood is identical with the being of the phenomenon, and then he proceeded to show that Husserl's "eidetic reduction" and Heidegger's "surpassing toward the ontological" do not lead us to the being of the phenomenon (EN, 15; BN, 7–8). Since in that section Sartre ultimately took Heidegger's "surpassing toward the ontological" as a way that leads to the phenomenon of being, we might think that Husserl's "eidetic reduction" is also a way that leads to the phenomenon of being. Moreover, in some places, Sartre took the phenomenon of being as "the meaning of the being of the existent in so far as it reveals [discloses] itself to consciousness" (EN, 30; BN, 25) and he took the meaning of the existent (object) as the essence of the existent (EN, 15; BN, 8). These seem to suggest that the phenomenon of being is simply the essence of the existent. But did Sartre really equate the phenomenon of being with the Husserlian essence? Let's consider the question carefully.

Section II of the *Introduction* to *Being and Nothingness* consists of three paragraphs: In the first paragraph, Sartre raised the question whether the phenomenon of being is the being of the phenomenon (EN, 14–15; BN, 7–8). In the second, Sartre argued that the being of the phenomenon is neither the Husserlian essence nor reached by the Heideggerian surpassing toward the ontological, where he took the being of the phenomenon as the condition of the disclosure of the phenomenon of being (as well as of any other phenomenon) (EN, 15; BN, 8). In the third, Sartre concluded that the being of the phenomenon is not the phenomenon of being (EN, 15–16; BN, 8–9). Now, what is the relation between the first and second paragraphs? In other words, why does the discussion of Husserl's views concerning the relation between the concrete phenomenon and the essence have anything do with the question whether the phenomenon of being is the being of the phenomenon?

One possible answer is just what we said above, that Husserl's essence and Heidegger's surpassing toward the ontological are or lead toward the phenomenon of being, and thus an examination of the issue whether

Husserl's essence or Heidegger's surpassing toward the ontological is or discloses the being of the phenomenon would help us determine whether the phenomenon of being is the being of the phenomenon. However, a close look at the text will show that this reading is wrong.

In the beginning of the first paragraph Sartre said: "Is it itself [the being of the appearance] an appearance? It seems so at first" (EN, 14; BN, 7). In the third paragraph of that section, Sartre said: "By not considering being as the condition of revelation [disclosure] but rather being as an appearance which can be determined in concepts, we have understood first of all that knowledge can not [cannot] by itself give an account of being; that is, the being of the phenomenon can not [cannot] be reduced to the phenomenon of being" (EN, 16; BN, 9). These remarks clearly suggest that Sartre initially took being (the being of the phenomenon) as an appearance, at the beginning of the section. Moreover, in the first paragraph, the only place Sartre talked about being when he attempted a Husserlian and a Heideggerian understanding of being, as he said: ". . . , is the being which discloses itself to me, which *appears to* me, of the same nature as the being of existents which appear to me? It seems that there is no difficulty. Husserl has shown how an eidetic reduction is always possible; that is, how one can always pass beyond the concrete phenomenon toward its essence. For Heidegger also 'human reality' is ontic-ontological; that is, it can always pass beyond the phenomenon toward its being" (EN, 14–15; BN, 7). In the above quoted passage it seems that the allusion to Husserl's and Heidegger's accounts was made as an initial "plausible" understanding of the being of the phenomenon, which (understanding) was supposed to be corrected later.

Additional evidence is found in the question raised near the end of the first paragraph: "Is passing beyond the existent toward the phenomenon of being actually to pass beyond it toward *its* being, as one passes beyond the particular red toward its essence?" (EN, 15; BN, 7–8). The question is whether passing beyond the existent toward the phenomenon of being is actually to pass beyond it toward its being, like what we see in passing beyond the particular red toward its essence. And the question presupposes that the passing beyond the particular red toward its essence is an instance of passing beyond the existent toward its being. Here, clearly, the essence is not equated with the phenomenon of being, for otherwise the question would become completely trivial and Sartre would not think the question worthy of further consideration. If the phenomenon of being were taken as the Husserlian essence, and the passing beyond the particular red toward its essence is an instance of passing beyond the existent toward its being, it is trivial that passing beyond the existent toward the phenomenon of being is to pass it toward its being. Thus, the phenomenon of being is not the Husserlian essence; it is rather the disclosure of the being-in-itself in boredom and nausea.

If my analysis above is correct, in the first paragraph of *section II*, both Husserl's eidetic reduction and Heidegger's surpassing were taken as a way leading to the being of the phenomenon. The reason Sartre mentioned Husserl's and Heidegger's accounts is not that he viewed their accounts as providing an explanation for the phenomenon of being. Rather, it is that he viewed their accounts as providing an explanation for the being of the phenomenon.

Finally, let me address the epistemological question how we can know anything about the being-in-itself. We know that, for Sartre, the three properties of the in-itself—the in-itself is in-itself; the in-itself is what it is; and the it-itself is—are disclosed to us in the phenomenon of being (EN, 30; BN, 24–25). And we also know that, for Sartre, the existence of the in-itself is demonstrated only through consulting the being of the for-itself (through "pure reflection"[29]) (EN, 27–29; BN, 21–24). But how can we know that what the phenomenon of being discloses is *the properties of the in-itself* rather than *the properties of something else* if the being of the in-itself is not disclosed in the phenomenon of being?

It seems to me that there is no easy way to answer this question. It does not help to say that we find analogous properties of the in-itself in non-positional consciousness. For even if we can pin down the properties of the in-itself through purely reflecting on the non-positional consciousness, and even if those properties are similar to the properties disclosed in the phenomenon of being, we still cannot be *certain* that the properties disclosed in the phenomenon of being are the properties of the in-itself rather than the properties of something else that happens to have properties similar to those of the in-itself.

Nothingness

It is no doubt true that for Sartre "nothingness" means the being of consciousness. However, "nothingness" also has other meanings—*négatités* (EN, 58; BN, 56), imagined objects (PI, 263), and perceptual objects (EN, 235; BN, 256–57). In this section, let me look at these meanings of nothingness and their relations.

Sartre first discussed nothingness at length in *The Psychology of Imagination*. There, nothingness was taken to be an imagined object.[30] And the imagined object—the nothingness—must, in one way or another, draw its source from the real world: Either it refers to something that exists in the world (e.g., Bill Clinton), or it consists of parts that exist in the world (e.g., a centaur) (PI, 268–73). Note that an imagined object is neither a hidden perceptual object, nor an anticipated or a recollected object or event. It is not a hidden perceptual object, since an imagined object appears only from a break from the reality as a whole,[31] whereas a hidden perceptual object, e.g., the back of the computer in front of which I am now sitting, although it does not show itself to me right now, is a potential part of my future perceptual experience, and henceforth a part of the reality as a whole (PI, 262). It is not an anticipated or a recollected object or event, since an imagined object appears as being isolated from the causal nexus of the world,[32] whereas an anticipated or a recollected object or event is causally connected with our current perceptual object or event (PI, 263–64).

In *The Psychology of Imagination*, the imaginary was said to appear "on the foundation of the world," and it "represents at each moment the implicit meaning of the real" (PI, 272–73). Moreover, for Sartre the negation is found *only* in the imaginary—it is embedded in the nature of an imagined object.[33] The ideas behind these claims are quite simple: The real, the realm of perceptual objects, is totally positive, and perceiving an object entails affirming the existence of the object. We don't find anything negative in reality. The imaginary, however, is both secondary to the real and contains the source of negation. It is secondary to the real, because an imagined object is modeled after the real and it is posited only on the condition that we *have perceived* the object or parts of the object (e.g., we can imagine Peter only on the condition that we have had perceptual contact with Peter in one way or another). It contains the source of negation, because whenever an imagined object appears, our attention is steered away from the real, and the imagined object appears to us as something that does not exist, something that is completely different from the real object. In other words, unlike the positive reality, the imaginary is negative, insofar as it contains within itself an implicit negation—the annihilation of the real.

In *Being and Nothingness*, however, Sartre held a *different* view about negation. There, negation was taken as having a primary source in *négatités*, the negative realities,[34] what he called "nothingness" in the chapter on the origin of negation (EN, 58; BN, 56). In other words, in *Being and Nothingness*, the real is not totally positive—there are negative realities such as the absence of Peter (EN, 44; BN, 40–41) and the destruction of beings (EN, 42–43; BN, 39). Sartre's motivation for introducing *négatitiés* in *Being and Nothingness* is quite clear—he wanted to use *négatitiés* as a leading thread to the for-itself and to the disclosure of the for-itself as nothingness. And he achieved this through two steps: 1. By making the distinction between negative reality as what is-not and positive reality as what is (EN, 57; BN, 55), Sartre claimed that negative realities—nothingness—are made-to-be. And hence, it is only through consciousness that negative realities can ever come to the world (insofar as the in-itself cannot cause and support anything). 2. Since negative realities contain negations, and consciousness is responsible for the occurrences of negative realities, consciousness must itself involve negation, insofar as a being full of positivity cannot support negation. In the following let me argue that both Sartre's motivation for introducing *négatitiés* and Sartre's step for realizing his goal are problematic.

First, it causes unnecessary complication to use *négatitiés* as a guiding thread to the for-itself as the original nothingness. To lead to the for-itself as Sartre desired in the chapter on the origin of nothingness, all we need is something that contains negation within itself. Clearly ordinary perceptual objects, the positive realities such as chairs, tables, etc., suffice, since positive realities "retain negation as the condition of the sharpness of their outlines, as that which fixes them as what they are" (EN, 57; BN, 55). Indeed, Sartre claimed in *chapter three* of *part two* of *Being and Nothingness* that all perceptual objects (e.g., an inkwell) are "nothingness," insofar as they have determinations that involve external negations of other objects (e.g., an inkwell is not a table) (EN, 235; BN, 256–57). If positive realities also involve negations and can be used as a guiding thread to the for-itself as the original nothingness, why should we bother to choose the more difficult route of positing *négatitiés*?

Second, Sartre's step for realizing his goal is problematic. In the first step, Sartre drew a distinction between negative reality as what is-not and positive reality as what is. How should we understand this distinction? It does not suffice that we observe that the positive reality (e.g., Peter) has a determinate shape whereas negative reality (e.g., absence of Peter) does not, since the determination of shape has nothing to do with existence or non-existence. It does not suffice either that we observe that the in-itself is the condition for the disclosure of positive reality, for the in-itself is the condition for the disclosure of negative reality too. The proper way to understand this distinction, it seems to me, is this: When we perceive positive reality (e.g., Peter), we posit the existence of something with a determinate shape (e.g., Peter); but when we perceive negative reality (e.g., absence of Peter), we do not posit the existence of anything with a determinate shape; rather, we posit the non-existence of an imagined object (e.g., an image of Peter). Thus, to understand the "is-not" character of negative reality, we need to understand the double negations embedded in our perception of negative reality: (1) the negation manifested in the nature of the imagined object (which object is denied in our perception of negative reality) as we discussed before; and (2) the negation manifested in perceiving (i.e., we do not *perceive* the imagined object at the very moment). Now, since the negation manifested in negative reality is in part reduced to the negation manifested in the nature of the imagined object, we need an account of imagination to support the theory of negative reality. However, in *Being and Nothingness*, Sartre could not appeal to the theory of imagination he proposed in *The Psychology of Imagination*, because in *Being and Nothingness* he could not accept the thesis that the imaginary is modeled after the real—the imagined objects are or are made of "annihilated" real objects. For if Sartre did accept it, and if the imaginary is modeled after the real, there should have been imagined *négatitiés*. But it is extraordinarily difficult to imagine the *négatitiés* by themselves, apart from a context (e.g., *the absence of Peter in general*). Thus, the first step is problematic, since Sartre didn't have a satisfactory account of *négatitiés*.

The Paradoxical Doctrine of Consciousness

The last item I would like to discuss in this chapter is Sartre's famous paradoxical doctrine that consciousness is not what it is and is what it is not, a doctrine he frequently referred to in *Being and Nothingness*. However, this doctrine does not have a univocal sense in *Being and Nothingness*. As one might expect, when Sartre went deeper and deeper into his investigations, the content of this doctrine became richer and richer. As far as I see it, this doctrine has at least four different senses in *Being and Nothingness*:

1. The doctrine was used to characterize the "internal negation," the ontological relation between the for-itself and the in-itself. In the *Introduction* to *Being and Nothingness*, we see a preliminary elucidation of the

doctrine in this sense, that from the general standpoint of intentionality, "consciousness is born supported by a being which is not itself" (EN, 28; BN, 23). We will discuss this sense of the doctrine in chapters 2 and 3.

2. The doctrine was used to characterize the human freedom that separates our current project and behavior from our past or future project and behavior. When Sartre discussed the vertigo example and the gambler example (EN, 67–69, 69–71; BN, 66–69, 69–70), he enriched the meaning of the paradoxical doctrine by claiming that consciousness is its future (what it is not yet) and is not its past (what it was). Although Sartre used difficult technical terms in illustration, the idea he tried to convey is quite simple: Our *current* decisions concerning our future selves *do not* really bind us as soon as the "now" is passed by.

3. The doctrine was used to characterize the relation between the for-itself and its intentional object in a project of "making to be the in-itself." Sartre discussed this sense of the doctrine mainly in the chapter on "bad faith" in *Being and Nothingness*, where he treated the relation between the for-itself and its intentional object as a presupposition of bad faith. We will discuss this sense of the doctrine in the section "The First Presupposition of Bad Faith," in chapter 4.

4. The doctrine was used to characterize the non-positional consciousness as a self-denying project in *section III* of the chapter on bad faith and in *chapter one* of *part two* of *Being and Nothingness*. We will discuss this sense of the doctrine in the section "The Second Presupposition of Bad Faith," in chapter 4.

In the foregoing, I have clarified some basic notions and doctrines in Sartre's early philosophy, which should prepare the ground for our further study. In the next chapter, I will discuss a fundamental element in Sartre's ontological project—his peculiar understanding of the doctrine of intentionality in *Being and Nothingess*—in comparison with Husserl's understanding of the doctrine of intentionality.

Notes

1.   Barring the special case of pure reflection, a consciousness cannot take itself as its intentional object. It is "irreflexive."

2.   In the English edition there are thirty-five occurrences of 'unreflected': It occurs in p. 41, line 9; p. 45, lines 13 and 25; p. 46, lines 6, 10, 17, and 23; p. 47,

line 7; p. 48, lines 1, 4, 20, and 27; p. 53, lines 7 and 15; p. 55, lines 23 and 27; p. 57, lines 1, 2, 14, and 24–25; p. 58, lines 1, 2, 7, 10, 24, and 27; p. 59, line 2; p. 60, line 1; p. 61, line 5; p. 65, line1; p. 74, line 21; p. 88, line 26; p. 89, line 9; p. 90, line 2; and p. 91, line 9.

3. What Sartre meant by "knowledge" is a cognitive, linguistic, *positional* consciousness (EN, 20; BN, 14). Hereinafter let me use 'knowledge*' to designate the Sartrean "knowledge."

4. I will discuss "bad faith" in chapter 4.

5. I will discuss "authenticity" in chapters 6 and 7.

6. I will discuss "pure reflection" in chapter 5.

7. E.g., see David Detmer, *Freedom as a Value: A Critique of the Ethical Theory of Jean-Paul Sartre* (La Salle, Ill.: Open Court, 1986), 20–22; Thomas Busch, *The Power of Consciousness and the Forms of Circumstances in Sartre's Philosophy* (Bloomington, Ind.: Indiana University Press, 1990), 7–8; Ronald Santoni, *Bad Faith, Good Faith, and Authenticity in Sartre's Early Philosophy* (Philadelphia: Temple University Press, 1995), 3–4.

8. E.g., at one place Jeffrey Gordon suggested that non-positional consciousness be periphery consciousness—the implicit consciousness of one's surrounding environment (Jeffrey Gordon, "Bad Faith: A Dilemma," *Philosophy* 60 [1985]: 258–62).

9. Kathleen Wider, *The Bodily Nature of Consciousness* (Ithaca, N.Y.: Cornell University Press, 1997), 112–49.

10. When we talk about the sides of consciousness, we take consciousness as a combination of the non-positional consciousness (the being of consciousness) and the intentional object.

11. See Sartre, PI, 14–15; TL, 23–24; TE, 40; EN, 17–21; BN, 11–15.

12. I owe this term to Paul Spade.

13. Wider, *Bodily Nature*, 116.

14. Wider, *Bodily Nature*, 115–18.

15. At one place my account seems to be at odds with Sartre's. Sartre held the "co-givenness thesis" that a consciousness is both an acquaintance (positional consciousness) and a "feel" (non-positional consciousness). I think there are problems with this thesis. On the one hand, one might object that a long-distance truck driver, after driving for a long period of time, has positional consciousness but is not non-positionally aware (of) anything (see Wider, *Bodily Nature*, 97–99). Thus, some acquaintances are not accompanied by "feels." On the other hand, it seems to me that we can be non-positionally aware (of) pleasure without being positionally aware of any object that causes the pleasure. Thus, some "feels" are not accompanied by acquaintances. However, there is a way to explain away the difference between Sartre's account and mine. Given that the consciousnesses Sartre was interested in studying in *Being and Nothingness* were only project-related consciousnesses, it is likely that what Sartre had in mind by the "co-givenness thesis" is the co-givenness of positional and non-positional consciousness *in a project-related consciousness.* (For a discussion of the notion of "project," see

chapter 3.) Qualified in this way, the co-givenness thesis is also true in my account.

16. By "mental act" I mean a concrete mental event.

17. By "the mind's moving from one state to another" I mean the flowing of consciousness, not the moments of transition of project-related acquaintances.

18. By "distinctive" I mean distinctive from other qualitative states or from other "feels."

19. Although many "feels" do not have *distinctive* qualities, they do have *some* quality, e.g., the quality of enabling us to make present-tense reports, which I will discuss in the next paragraph.

20. Although the project-related "feels" can be described in functional terms, the non-project-related "feels" cannot be described in functional terms.

21. 'Attending-to' and 'attended to' are my technical terms. They don't mean exactly the same things as they do in ordinary language or other philosophical contexts.

22. The word 'witnessing' is used in a special sense. It shouldn't be understood as indicating a subject/object split, i.e., the split between the agent that does the witnessing and what is witnessed. I am grateful to Zhenming Zhai for bringing this to my attention.

23. The element is time-sensitive in the sense that we witness it when we make present-tense reports, and we don't witness it when we make past-tense or future-tense reports.

24. Of course, in that case she is not those "feels" that accompany linguistic activities.

25. I will discuss the original ontological relation in chapters 2 and 3.

26. "[T]he world and the instrumental-thing, space and quantity, and universal time are all pure hypostasized nothingnesses which in no way modify the pure being which is revealed through them" (EN, 269; BN, 296). See also EN, 15; BN, 8.

27. I will discuss "the condition of disclosure" in chapter 3.

28. "Being will be disclosed to us by some kind of immediate access —boredom, nausea, *etc.*" (EN, 14; BN, 7).

29. I will discuss "pure reflection" at length in chapter 3 and chapter 5.

30. For example, if I imagine Peter, in the imaginary consciousness Peter is nothingness. "But if I imagine Peter as he might be at that moment in Berlin—or simply Peter as he exists at the moment (and not as he was yesterday on leaving me), I grasp an object which is not at all given to me or which is given to me simply as being beyond reach. There I grasp *nothing*, that is, I posit *nothingness*" (PI, 263).

31. In this sense an "imaginative act is . . . *annihilating*" (PI, 263).

32. In this sense an "imaginative act is . . . *isolating*" (PI, 263).

33. See PI, 272–73: "The imaginative act itself consists in positing the imaginary for itself, that is, in making that meaning explicit—as when Peter as an image rises suddenly before me—but this specific position of the imaginary will be accompanied by a collapsing of the world, which is then no more than the negated foundation of the unreal. And if the negation is the unconditioned principle of all imagination, it itself can never be realized excepting in and by an act of imagina-

tion."

34. Of course, the negative realities are different from imagined objects; e.g., the absence of Peter in a perception is different from the same Peter in an image.

Chapter Two

Sartre versus Husserl: A Study of the Doctrine of Intentionality

Introduction

It is a commonly held opinion that Sartre, following Husserl, adopted a constitutional version of the doctrine of intentionality, i.e., consciousness is consciousness *of* its intentional object in the sense that consciousness constitutes its intentional object out of certain raw material. According to this opinion, the only difference between Sartre and Husserl with respect to the doctrine of intentionality is that, for Sartre, the raw material is the mind-independent being-in-itself, whereas for Husserl it comes from consciousness.[1]

This opinion, in spite of its admirable simplicity, is at odds with what Sartre said in *section V* of *Introduction* to *Being and Nothingness*:

> All consciousness is consciousness *of* something. This definition of consciousness can be taken in two very distinct senses: either we understand by this that consciousness is constitutive of the being of its object, or it means that consciousness in its inmost nature is a relation to a transcendent being. But the first interpretation of the formula destroys itself. . . . For Husserl, for example, the animation of the hyletic nucleus by the only intentions which can find their fulfillment (*Erfüllung*) in this *hyle* is not enough to bring us outside of subjectivity. . . . Husserl defines consciousness precisely as a transcendence. In truth he does. This is what he posits. This is his essential discovery. But from the moment that he makes of the *noema* an *unreal*, a correlate *of* the *noesis*, a noema whose *esse* is *percipi*, he is totally unfaithful to his principle. (EN, 27–28; BN, 21–23)

In the above passage Sartre distinguished two versions of the doctrine of intentionality: the constitutional version, which he attributed to Husserl and which he rejected; and his own version, which I call the "ontological" version, whose sense will be explained below in the third section. Upon a close look at Sartre's early works, I argue that the common opinion is not entirely true; the difference between Sartre and Husserl goes far beyond the one recognized by that opinion. Although Sartre did accept the doctrine of intentionality in his early works, he didn't take the doctrine in a single sense, and moreover, in *Being and Nothingness*, Sartre took the doctrine in a sense different from Husserl's and from his own earlier constitutional version in *The Transcendence of the Ego*.

Husserl's Constitutional Version of Intentionality

Its medieval origin set aside, the doctrine of intentionality can be traced back to Franz Brentano. According to Brentano, intentionality is the feature that distinguishes the psychological phenomenon from the physical phenomenon. It is understood as the fact that in every psychological phenomenon—love, hatred, perception, imagination—consciousness is always "directed at" a certain intentional object. Here by "directedness" Brentano meant an "*existential*" bond between consciousness and its intentional object; "*existential*," that is to say, the intentional object appears to consciousness through our living the consciousness and losing ourselves to the object. For example, suppose I am reading an interesting novel and absorbed in the story. The intentional object I have in my reading is the story, and the story is apprehended through my living the reading consciousness.

There is no question that Brentano's doctrine of intentionality deeply influenced Husserl. In *Logical Investigations*, Husserl faithfully followed Brentano in espousing the existential version of intentionality.[2] However, from *The Idea of Phenomenology* onwards, Husserl launched a new understanding of the doctrine of intentionality, according to which:

Each *cogito*, each conscious process, we may also say, *"means"* something or other and bears in itself, in this manner peculiar to the *meant*, its particular *cogitatum*. Each does this, moreover, in its own fashion. The house-perception means a house—more precisely, as this individual house—and means it in the fashion peculiar to perception; a house-memory means a house in the fashion peculiar to memory; a house-phantasy, in the fashion peculiar to phantasy. . . . Conscious processes are also called *intentional*; but then the word intentionality signifies nothing else than this universal fundamental property of consciousness: to be consciousness of something; as a *cogito*, to bear within itself its *cogitatum*.[3]

By saying that a *cogito* bears within itself its *cogitatum*, Husserl certainly did not mean that the *cogitatum* is a genuine part of the *cogito*, but that in order for the *cogito* to be understood as "meaning" we must have the "meant" (*cogitatum* qua *cogitatum*) *as a conceptual correlate*. At the outset we may raise the following questions: What did Husserl mean by "meaning" and "meant" in this context? Is this meaning/meant relation—a *conceptual* bond—a faithful reformulation or a parallel reconstruction of the "directedness" of consciousness to its intentional object in the existential version of intentionality? Let's consider these questions closely.

First of all, when Husserl discussed the conceptual bond, the meaning/meant relation, he had something definite in mind. The *cogito*, the "meaning," is a combination of the "synthesizing" principle and certain hyletic material, where "synthesis" is defined as "[t]he sort of combination uniting consciousness with consciousness."[4] The *cogitatum*, the "meant," is *not* the intentional object to which we lose ourselves in an unreflective consciousness, but *the cogitatum qua cogitatum, the signification of the object with respect to the cogito*. Let me elaborate on the two correlates.

First, let me discuss the *cogito*. In *The Idea of Phenomenology, Ideas I, and Cartesian Meditations*, consciousness (or "*cogitatio*") was first introduced as a conscious act, a common non-complex mental process.[5] But then, at some later stages, a mental process became a complex of the *cogito* (or "*noesis*") and the *cogitatum* (or "*noema*"). Having the *cogito* as the really inherent moment, a mental process was understood as a combination of the synthesizing principle governed by a rule[6] and of the momentary appearance.[7] We will evaluate this move later, but at present let me present Husserl's view of the *cogito* in connection with what he called "sensualism."[8] According to Husserl, sensualism takes a *cogito* as a certain mixture of "form" and some external or internal sensory data.[9] Although Husserl agreed with the sensualists about the division between sensory data and something that "operates" on data, he disagreed with the sensualists about the process of the "operation": For sensualists, form is like a molder that shapes the data, whereas for Husserl synthesis involves not only the current sensory appearance, but also the past and future appearances. In other words, unlike sensualists' data-independent forms, Husserl's synthesizing principle refers to a "horizon," a series of infinite potential appearances that can never be fully had and determined by any human being.[10]

Next, let me discuss the *cogitatum*. The *cogitatum*, as the correlate of the *cogito*, is what is meant by, and the corresponding result of, applying a synthesizing principle to appearances. Here notice two things:

1. The *cogitatum* is *not* the intentional object grasped in an unreflective consciousness; it is rather the meaning of the intentional object understood in relation to the *cogito*. In other words, the *cogitatum* is neither a real object (in this world) nor an imaginary object (in a possible world) that we are positionally aware of in an unreflective consciousness. Rather, it is what is meant at the object-pole in correlation to our applying a synthesizing principle to appearances—a reconstructed parallel of the intentional object.

2. The *cogitatum* "transcends" the *cogito* not in the common sense that the *cogitatum* is external to and has no dependence on the *cogito*, but in the sense that the *cogito* as the meaning refers to something meant, something that is not the synthesizing principle, that is beyond appearances, and that serves as a bearer that binds together infinite appearances.[11] In other words, since the *cogito*—our applying a synthesizing principle to appearances—can be understood as an intending beyond appearances, the *cogitatum*—the correlate of the *cogito* at the object-pole—must be different from mere appearances. It is in this sense we should understand Husserl's remark that the *cogitatum* is "the transcendent object within the immanence."[12] The *cogitatum* is within the immanence, since it is the meant that cannot be understood separately from the meaning; and yet it is transcendent, since it is beyond the momentary appearances.

This said, we see that the conceptual bond between the *cogito* and the *cogitatum* is really a *constitutional* bond; *constitutional*, that is to say, the *cogitatum* is understood as the constituted result of the *cogito*, and the *cogito* a constituting complex consisting of a synthesizing principle and appearances. This constitutional version of intentionality differs from Brentano's existential version in the following four aspects (the consciousness in the existential version corresponds to the *cogito* in the constitutional version, and the intentional object in the existential version corresponds to the *cogitatum* in the constitutional version):

1. In the existential version, there is no evidence that consciousness is understood as a complex mental act, whereas in the constitutional version the *cogito* is understood as a complex consisting of a synthesizing principle and appearances.

2. In the existential version, the intentional object (in an unreflective consciousness) is normally the everyday, worldly object; whereas in the constitutional version, the *cogitatum qua cogitatum* is the "object" as meant, a theoretical entity that we never encounter in everyday life.

3. In the existential version, the bond between consciousness and its intentional object is a simple, existential one, whereas in the constitutional version, the bond between the *cogito* and the *cogitatum* is a constitutional one.

4. In the existential version, the intentional object transcends consciousness in the sense that the object we grasp and to which we lose ourselves is simply external to and has no ontological dependence on the very conscious act in which we grasp the object, whereas in the constitutional version, the *cogitatum* transcends the *cogito* in the sense that the *cogitatum* is beyond the inherent moments of the *cogito* to which the *cogitatum* is essentially related.

Having explained Husserl's constitutional version of intentionality, let me evaluate it through critically examining, from Sartre's point of view, a crucial move Husserl took, the move that the *cogito*—the really inherent moment of a mental process—is taken as a combination of a synthesizing principle and momentary appearances.

To say that the momentary appearances are a part of the *cogito* is to say that consciousness has an unconscious component. The reason is that in any consciousness we are not non-positionally aware (of) the momentary appearances, whereas we are non-positionally aware (of) the *cogito*. At the non-positional side, our "feel" might be the *flowing* of our conscious act but it is never the momentary appearances. Suppose I stare at the sun. My "feel" is the burning of my eyes, but not the appearance of the sun. Suppose I perceive a cube through looking at it from various angles. My "feel" is the flowing of my sense experience, but not a series of the momentary appearances of the cube. Now, if one believes in the translucency of consciousness, as Sartre did, she will disapprove the inclusion of momentary appearances in the *cogito*.

If the claim that consciousness has an unconscious component of the momentary appearances is unacceptable to those who believe the translucency of consciousness, the claim that *cogito* in general involves a synthesizing principle is wrong for everyone, for the following reason. The claim that *cogito* in general involves a synthesizing principle implies that any unreflective *cogito* involves a synthesizing principle. Suppose this implied claim is true. Then the synthesizing principle is either a conscious part[13] or an unconscious part of the *cogito*. But the synthesizing principle cannot be an unconscious part of the *cogito*, since (1) it is supposed to function as the active, constituting process of the *cogito*, and (2) something *active* in the *cogito* cannot be an unconscious part of the *cogito*. Thus the synthesizing principle can only be a conscious part of the *cogito*—a part that is self-consciously lived. But what would a consciousness that involves a self-consciously lived synthesizing principle be like? Well, if we are to live that consciousness, we must, in that consciousness, grasp the appearances as the object of positional consciousness, for otherwise the synthesizing principle would apply to nothing, and it would not be self-consciously lived. However, in any ordinary unreflective consciousness, the object of our positional consciousness is anything but the momentary appearances.[14] Hence, the unreflective *cogito* cannot be an ordinary unreflective consciousness, although it is supposed to be an ordinary unreflective consciousness. Thus, we get an absurdity. So, our supposition is false, and the claim that an unreflective *cogito* involves a synthesizing principle is wrong. Accordingly, the claim that *cogito* in general involves a synthesizing principle is wrong.

Sartre's Ontological Version of Intentionality in *Being and Nothingness*

Having examined Husserl's constitutional version of intentionality, let's turn to Sartre's ontological version.

First, we should observe that before *Being and Nothingness*, Sartre accepted (or at least didn't explicitly reject) Husserl's constitutional version of intentionality. In *The Transcendence of Ego*, Sartre devoted a chapter to the discussion of the constitution of the ego in a more or less Husserlian line[15] (TL, 44–74; TE, 60–93). In *The Psychology of Imagination*, Sartre drew a distinction between the physical or mental content of an image[16] and the imagined object, which bears at least *prima facie* similarity to Husserl's distinction between the appearances and the noematic objects (PI, 25).[17] It is not until the time of *Being and Nothingness* that Sartre explicitly rejected his earlier Husserlian constitutional version of intentionality, where Sartre criticized Husserl's and his own earlier constitutional version and presented an alternate ontological version of intentionality (EN, 27–28, 219–71; BN, 21–23, 238–98). In this section, I would like to focus on two questions: 1. What is Sartre's ontological version of intentionality as he presented it in *Being and Nothingness*? 2. How is the change (from his earlier constitutional version to the ontological version) possible? Let me consider the second question first.

We know that one of the main theses in *The Transcendence of the Ego* is that the transcendental ego does not belong to consciousness. And Sartre's major argument for the thesis runs as follows:

Premise 1: Every consciousness has two sides—the positional side and the non-positional side, and the being of a consciousness is characterized by its non-positional side (TL, 23–24; TE, 40–41).
Premise 2: If the transcendental ego does belong to consciousness, it must be found at the non-positional side of consciousness, i.e., we must be non-positionally aware (of) the transcendental ego (TL, 23–24; TE, 40).
Premise 3: Non-positional consciousness leaves a non-thetic memory through which we can retrieve the past non-positional consciousness.[18]
Premise 4: By consulting the non-thetic memory, we find that we are not non-positionally aware (of) the transcendental ego.[19]
Conclusion: The transcendental ego does not belong to consciousness.

My purpose for bringing up the above argument is not to examine its soundness, but to show that Sartre *should have rejected* Husserl's constitutional version of intentionality in *The Transcendence of the Ego*, insofar as a slight modification of the above argument undercuts Husserl's claim that the momentary appearances belong to consciousness. The modified argument runs as follows:

Premise 1*: The same as Premise 1 above.
Premise 2*: If the momentary appearances do belong to consciousness, they must be found at the non-positional side of consciousness, i.e., we must be non-positionally aware (of) the momentary appearances.
Premise 3*: The same as Premise 3 above.
Premise 4*: By consulting the non-thetic memory, we find that we are not non-positionally aware (of) the momentary appearances.
Conclusion*: The momentary appearances do not belong to consciousness.

Note here that the modified argument has not only the same structure, but also premises of the same sort, as the original argument. In other words, the two arguments should have the same degree of plausibility. And if Sartre succeeded in refuting the inclusion of the transcendental ego in consciousness, he should have succeeded in refuting the inclusion of the momentary appearances in consciousness as well, had he thought of the modified argument. It is surprising that Sartre missed such an obvious modification of his argument, but in any case, we see that the root of Sartre's later rejection of the constitutional version of intentionality is already there in *The Transcendence of the Ego*.

Having answered the second question—how is the change from his earlier constitutional version to the ontological version possible—let me clarify Sartre's ontological version of intentionality in *Being and Nothingness*.

According to Sartre, the relation between the for-itself and its intentional object is derived from the original ontological relation "between"[20] the for-itself and the in-itself. For a perceptual object, its basic properties, e.g., individuality, spatiality, and temporality, are all derived from or modeled after the ontological relation "between" the for-itself and the in-itself (EN, 235–68; BN, 257–94). For an imagined object, its properties are derived either from those of the correlated perceptual object or from those of its component parts that are themselves derived from perceptual objects. The ontological relation "between" the for-itself and the in-itself is the nucleus of Sartre's theory of intentionality.

Note that the ontological relation "between" the for-itself and the in-itself is not an external relation that is added to the for-itself and the in-itself. Rather, it is internal to the being of consciousness. In fact, the being of consciousness is the ontological relation to the in-itself (EN, 224; BN, 244); i.e., we are non-positionally aware (of) the ontological relation. In *chapter three* of *part two* of *Being and Nothingness*, Sartre called this ontological relation "internal negation."

A detailed discussion of "internal negation" will be given later in chapter 3. At present, let me make some preliminary observations of the ontological relation "between" the for-itself and the in-itself through an example.

Consider a knowing consciousness, e.g., a perception of a table. In the perception, we are positionally aware of the table and non-positionally aware (of) our perceiving the table (in contrast to imagining the table, recollecting the table, or imagining, recollecting something else). If we look closely at the non-positional "feel" (of) perceiving the table, we find several negative aspects that might help illustrate the ontological relation "between" the for-itself and the in-itself.

1. The "feel" (of) perceiving the table can be understood as a disclosure

of the table. Because the in-itself is the condition of all disclosure (EN, 15; BN, 8), and because the "feel" (of) perceiving the table characterizes the being of the perceptual for-itself, the for-itself as a disclosing consciousness presupposes and hence is not identical to the in-itself.

2. The "feel" (of) perceiving the table can be understood as a project of not-being the table. If the for-itself is to be a table, it must shut down all its thoughts and become self-identical. But by perceiving the table and by being non-positionally aware (of) perceiving the table, the for-itself engages itself in a project that presupposes and exemplifies non-self-identity. Hence, the for-itself "is not" the in-itself in the sense that the non-positional "feel" (of) perceiving the table presupposes and exemplifies non-self-identity.

3. The "feel" (of) perceiving the table is for Sartre a project of the for-itself's presenting itself to itself (EN, 115–21; BN, 119–26). But to present itself to itself, the for-itself must *distinguish* itself from something else; otherwise it cannot "know" that what it is non-positionally aware (of) is *itself* rather than any other thing or simply nothing. In perceiving the table, the for-itself establishes that the "feel" (of) perceiving the table is itself by distinguishing the "feel" from a co-present object which is not itself—the table as the disclosure of the in-itself.[21]

If my foregoing observations are correct, some further questions might be raised:

1. If the being of consciousness is a relation to the in-itself, isn't consciousness a non-self-sufficient moment, a mere abstraction of what Sartre called the ὅλον (EN, 716; BN, 791)—the totality of the for-itself and the in-itself?

2. If the answer to the first question is "yes"—that is, the ontological category of the for-itself is simply not a category of self-sufficient being—why is for-itself a fundamental ontological category and how did Sartre determine ontological categories?

To the first question, Sartre's answer is affirmative. Because consciousness is internally bound to the in-itself by the ontological relation, consciousness is "articulated with the in-itself so as to constitute a totality" (EN, 716; BN, 790), a unitary synthesis of the for-itself and the in-itself, the ὅλον(EN, 716; BN, 791). Thus, consciousness considered apart is only an abstraction—"it could not exist any more than a color could exist without form or a sound without pitch and without timbre" (EN, 716; BN, 790). In other words, consciousness is not a self-sufficient being, and the only self-sufficient beings are the in-itself and the ὅλον(EN, 715–16; BN, 790–91).

Now, how did Sartre determine ontological categories? Obviously, Sartre didn't appeal to self-sufficiency, because self-sufficiency is neither a sufficient nor a necessary condition for something to be counted as an ontological category. Self-sufficiency is not a sufficient condition for something to be counted as an ontological category, because the ὅλον is self-sufficient, but not an ontological category. It is not a necessary condition, because consciousness is an ontological category but not self-sufficient. How exactly did Sartre determine ontological categories?

With respect to the for-itself, its being is established in terms of its non-positional consciousness. With respect to the in-itself, its existence is proved by consulting the non-positional "feel" (of) the for-itself, and its properties—"the in-itself is in-itself," "the in-itself is what it is," "the in-itself is"—are disclosed in the positional consciousness of the phenomenon of being. *Thus, it is ultimately by appealing to his theory of non-positional consciousness that Sartre established the for-itself and the in-itself as two fundamental ontological categories.*

Because the in-itself is self-sufficient, whereas the for-itself is not, the in-itself has an ontological priority over the for-itself.[22] Because the existence of the in-itself is proven through our purely reflecting on the being of consciousness, the for-itself has a sort of epistemological priority over the in-itself.

Conclusion

Having presented Husserl's constitutional version and Sartre's ontological version of the doctrine of intentionality respectively, I have shown that although for Sartre consciousness is responsible for the positing of its intentional object, it does not constitute its intentional object in the same way the *cogito* constitutes the *cogitatum* in Husserl's account. Although their accounts share the weakness that they do not sufficiently appreciate the importance of this world,[23] Sartre's ontological account has an advantage of more easily explaining the transcendence of the intentional objects. In Husserl's account, since Husserl used the momentary appearance and the synthesizing principle to account for the *cogitatum*, he had a hard time explaining the transcendence of the intentional objects. In Sartre's account, however, there is no difficulty in accounting for the transcendence of the intentional objects, since perceptual objects are the disclosure of the in-itself.

Notes

1. Husserl called the raw stuff "hyletic material," which is a really inherent moment of a mental process. See Edmund Husserl, *Ideas Pertaining to a Pure Phenomenology and to a Phenomenological Philosophy*, trans. by F. Kersten (Martinus Nijhoff Publishers, 1983), 236–38.

2. See Roderick Chisholm, *Realism and the Background of Phenomenology* (Glencoe, Ill.: Free Press, 1960).

3. Edmund Husserl, *Cartesian Meditations*, trans. by Dorian Cairns (The Hague, Netherlands: Martinus Nijhoff, 1960), 33.

4. Husserl, *Cartesian Meditations*, 39. Here is an example to illustrate the synthesis of consciousness: "For example, if I take the perceiving of this die as the theme for my description, I see in pure reflection [not "pure reflection" in Sartre's sense] that 'this' die is given continuously as an objective unity in a multi-form and changeable multiplicity of manners of appearing, which belong determinately to it. These, in their temporal flow, are not an incoherent sequence of subjective processes. Rather they flow away in the unity of a synthesis, such that in them 'one and the same' is intended as appearing. The one identical die appears, now in 'near appearances', now in 'far appearances': in the changing modes of the Here and There, over against an always co-intended, though perhaps unheeded, absolute Here (in my co-appearing organism)" (Husserl, *Cartesian Meditations*, 39–40).

5. See Husserl, *Ideas*, 112–14; *The Idea of Phenomenology*, trans. by William Alston and George Nakhnikian (The Hague, Netherlands: Martinus Nijhoff, 1973), 23.

6. "The fact is that the constituting multiplicities of consciousness—those actually or possibly combined to make the unity of an identifying synthesis—are not accidental but, as regards the possibility of such a synthesis, *belong together for essential reasons*. Accordingly they are governed by *principles*, thanks to which our phenomenological investigations do not get lost in disconnected descriptions but are essentially organized. Any 'Objective' object, *any object whatever* (even an immanent one), points to *a structure, within the transcendental ego, that is governed by a rule*" (Husserl, *Cartesian Meditations*, 53). Incidentally, this rule is called "the principle of series" by Sartre in *Section I* of the *Introduction* to *Being and Nothingness*.

7. See Husserl, *Ideas*, 211–21; *The Idea of Phenomenology*, 43.

8. Note that "sensualism" in Dorion Cairns' translation has the wrong connotation in English that it has something to do with hedonic experience. In fact, if there were such a word, "sensuousism" would be a better translation insofar as it avoids hedonic connotations.

9.   Husserl, *Cartesian Meditations*, 38.

10.   "It becomes evident that, as intentional, the analysis of consciousness is totally different from analysis in the usual and natural sense. Conscious life, as we said once before, is not just a whole made up of 'data' of consciousness and therefore 'analyzable' (in an extremely broad sense, divisible) merely into its self-sufficient moment and non-self-sufficient *elements*—the form of unity (the 'form-qualities') being included then among the non-selfsufficient elements. To be sure, when regard is directed to certain themes, intentional "analysis" does lead *also* to such divisions, and to that extent the word can still serve the original sense; but everywhere its peculiar attainment (as "intentional") is an uncovering of the *potentialities "implicit"* in actualities of consciousness—an uncovering that brings about, on the noematic side, an "explication" or "unfolding", a "becoming distinct" and perhaps a "clearing" of what is consciously meant (the objective sense) and, correlatively, an explication of the potential intentional processes themselves" (Husserl, *Cartesian Meditations*, 46).

11.   "In our example, each phase of perception was a mere side of 'the' object, as what was perceptually meant. This *intending-beyond-itself*, which is implicit in any consciousness, must be considered an essential moment of it. That, on the other hand, this intending is, and must be, a 'meaning more' of the Same becomes shown only by the evidence of a possible making distinct and, ultimately, of an intuitive uncovering, in the form of actual and possible continued perceiving or of possible recollecting, as something to be done on my initiative" (Husserl, *Cartesian Meditations*, 46).

12.   ". . . the *cogitationes*, which we regard as simple data and in no way mysterious, hide all sorts of transcendencies. . . . that the phenomenon of sound perception, even as evident and reduced, demands within the immanent a distinction between *appearance* and *that which appears*. We thus have two absolute data, the givenness of the appearing and the givenness of the object; and the object within this immanence is not immanence in the sense of genuine immanence" (Husserl, *The Idea of Phenomenology*, 8–9).

13.   By "X's being a conscious part" I mean we are in some way (but not positionally) aware of X in an unreflective consciousness involving X.

14.   Even in many reflective consciousnesses, where we think *of* ourselves, our states, qualities, actions, etc., the positional object of our consciousness is not the momentary appearances.

15.   Although in *The Transcendence of the Ego* Sartre rejected Husserl's notion of "transcendental ego," he still accepted Husserl's distinction between the synthesizing principle and the appearances, and he accepted the general procedure of constitution.

16.   Note that, for Sartre, an "image" means an imaginary consciousness, not a mental picture that resembles a physical object (PI, 7–8).

17.   Upon a close look at *The Psychology of Imagination*, one may seriously doubt that Sartre really adopted Husserl's theory of constitution in accounting for

the nature of the images. Although Sartre did take an imagined object to be a result of a certain synthesis out of certain physical or mental content (PI, 29), his notion of "physical or mental content" is quite different from Husserl's "appearances": 1. Unlike the appearances, the physical or mental content of an image serves as an analogue of the imagined object (e.g., a photo of someone X is the physical content of an image of X, and the photo is an analogue of the person X). 2. Although physical or mental content provides a means through which the imagined object appears to consciousness ("our conclusion is that the image is an act which envisions an absent or non-existent object as a body, by means of a physical or mental content which is present only as an 'analogical representative' of the object envisioned" [PI, 26]), *physical or mental content does not really belong to the image*, since we are neither positionally aware of nor non-positionally aware (of) the content. That we are not positionally aware of the content is obvious, for in an image positionally, we are only aware of the imagined object. That we are not non-positionally aware (of) the content can be seen from the following argument: According to Sartre in *The Psychology of Imagination*, the physical content of an image is reconstructable from our thinking about the physical content *in a separate perceptual consciousness*, whereas the mental content of an image is in principle not reconstructable (PI, 76–77). This suggests that we are not non-positionally aware (of) the physical or mental content, for if we were, there would be no need to *reconstruct* or *try to reconstruct* the content, instead of simply retrieving the content, as it were, at the non-positional side. In sum, since Sartre's notion of "physical or mental content" is different from Husserl's "appearances," and since Sartre claimed that we cannot know anything about the mental content of an image (except that the content is a means through which the imagined object appears), Sartre lacked the appropriate ground that would enable him to have a Husserlian theory of constitution *for images*.

18. "But every unreflected consciousness, being non-thetic consciousness of itself, leaves a non-thetic memory that one can consult. To do so it suffices to try to reconstitute the complete moment in which this unreflected consciousness appeared (which by definition is always possible)" (TL, 30; TE, 46). I will discuss the notion of "non-thetic memory" at length in chapter 5.

19. ". . . while I was reading, there was consciousness *of* the book, *of* the heroes of the novel, but the *I* was not inhabiting this consciousness. It was only consciousness of the object and non-positional consciousness of itself. I can now make these a-thetically apprehended results the object of a thesis and declare: there was no I in the unreflected consciousness" (TL, 30; TE, 46–47).

20. I put 'between' in quotation marks because in the context of our discussion of the original ontological relation, it does not stand for an external relation.

21. "It is in fact in terms of the being which it is not that a being can *make known to itself* what it is not. This means, in the case of an internal negation, that it is within and upon the being which it is not that it is not that the for-itself appears as not being what it is not" (EN, 224–25; BN, 245).

22. "Thus the *ontological* problem of knowledge is resolved by the affirmation of the ontological primacy of the in-itself over the for-itself" (EN, 713; BN, 787).

23. In Husserl's account, by viewing consciousness as something not confined to positing objects of *this world*, Husserl put the real world on a par with any imaginary or merely possible world, and he treated seeing things as we do in this world (e.g., perceiving pain as pain) as not being preferable to seeing things in other possible ways (e.g., perceiving pain as the stimulation of C-fibers or as the manifestation of an evil god). In Sartre's account, although the consciousness Sartre discussed in *Being and Nothingness* is mainly perceptual consciousness, he never said that perceptual consciousness is the primary mode of consciousness.

Chapter Three

Freedom in Sartre's *Being and Nothingness*

Introduction

It is well known that there is an apparent inconsistency in Sartre's views about freedom in *Being and Nothingness*. While at many places Sartre stressed the absolute nature of freedom, as he said we are "absolutely free" (EN, 591; BN, 653), "totally free" (EN, 641; BN, 709), "wholly and forever free" (EN, 516; BN, 569), and "condemned to be free" (EN, 591; BN, 653), at other places he acknowledged the limitation of our freedom, as he claimed that our freedom is limited by the "circumstance"[1] and our facticity (EN, 561–638; BN, 619–707). Given the importance of the notion of freedom in Sartre's early philosophy, it is crucial to our understanding of Sartre whether this alleged inconsistency is a genuine one.

In this chapter, I argue that the alleged inconsistency is *not* a genuine one. I offer a new interpretation of freedom in Sartre's *Being and Nothingness*, on the basis of which interpretation I develop an account to resolve the alleged inconsistency. Moreover, I argue that my interpretation helps illuminate Sartre's ontological project in general, because it sheds light on two important notions, "internal negation" and "the ontological proof."

I shall start by criticizing a well-known account to resolve the alleged inconsistency, David Detmer's.

Criticism of Detmer's Account

Among the various accounts to resolve the alleged inconsistency, a common approach is to try to explain it away by neglecting or downplaying

Sartre's views about the limitation of freedom. Commentators such as Dagfinn Føllesdal,[2] Risieri Frondizi,[3] Walter Kaufmann,[4] Hubert Marcuse,[5] and Mary Warnock[6] all adopted this approach: In their accounts, they overlooked or downplayed the passages in which Sartre espoused and elaborated on the limitation of freedom. As a result, they equated Sartre's freedom with absolute freedom, which they further equated with unlimited freedom. Because this approach fails to do justice to the extensive texts in which Sartre discussed the limitation of freedom, I dismiss it without giving detailed arguments.

In his book *Freedom as a Value: A Critique of the Ethical Theory of Jean-Paul Sartre*,[7] David Detmer adopted a better approach. Detmer distinguished two sorts of freedom: "practical freedom" and "ontological freedom."[8] Practical freedom is the ability of obtaining the end chosen.[9, 10] For example, some but not all people have the practical freedom of becoming philosophers, because some people (such as those who are starving) have little time for philosophical thinking. Ontological freedom is the freedom of transcending one's circumstance* through various nihilating behaviors.[11] Everyone has the ontological freedom all the time, because no matter what circumstance* she is in, she can always go beyond the circumstance* by interpreting the circumstance*, setting up a goal, and so forth. On the basis of this distinction, Detmer argued that the alleged inconsistency can be resolved, because, according to his account, Sartre had in mind the ontological freedom while he was discussing the absolute nature of freedom, and the practical freedom while he was discussing the limitation of freedom.[12] Detmer's argument has two premises:

1. Sartre endorsed the distinction between ontological freedom and practical freedom in *Being and Nothingness*. And when Sartre claimed that our freedom is limited, he meant the limitation of *practical freedom* (in the sense that we are not omnipotent); and when he claimed that our freedom is absolute, he meant that our *ontological freedom*, the freedom of transcending our circumstance through various nihilating behaviors, has no limitation.

2. If the first premise is correct, the alleged inconsistency can be resolved.

I agree with Detmer on the second premise. However, I disagree with him on the first one. I have two arguments against Detmer's first premise.

First, Detmer's practical freedom was *not* considered by Sartre as one of his technical notions of "freedom" in *Being and Nothingness*.[13] In the chapter on freedom in *Being and Nothingness*, Sartre *denied* that he considered freedom to be practical freedom:

In addition it is necessary to point out to "common sense" that the formula "to be free" does not mean "to obtain what one has wished" but rather "by oneself to determine oneself to wish" (in the broad sense of choosing). In other words success is not important to freedom. The discussion which opposes common sense to philosophers stems here from a misunderstanding: the empirical and popular concept of "freedom" which has been produced by historical, political, and moral circumstances is equivalent to "the ability to obtain the end chosen." The technical and philosophical concept of freedom, the only one which we are considering here, means only the autonomy of choice. (EN, 563; BN, 621–22)

Because Detmer's practical freedom is the ability of obtaining the end chosen, it is "the empirical and popular concept of freedom" or "the freedom of obtaining" that Sartre chose *not to consider* in the above passage.

Second, as the ability of obtaining the end chosen, practical freedom is a *quality* to be possessed by a substance. But in *Being and Nothingness* Sartre insisted that freedom be the *being* of consciousness rather than a *quality* possessed by a substance. In the chapter on freedom, Sartre said: "[M]y freedom is perpetually in questions in my being; it is not a quality added on or a *property* of my nature. It is very exactly the stuff of my being" (EN, 514; BN, 566).

In *Being and Nothingness*, not only did Sartre *not* consider Detmer's practical freedom, but also, he had (or at least ended up with) only *one* notion of freedom. He said: "[T]he technical and philosophical concept, the only one which we are considering here, means only the autonomy of choice" (EN, 563; BN, 622). By "here" Sartre referred to the chapter on freedom. Because the chapter on freedom contains Sartre's most detailed discussions and final views of freedom in *Being and Nothingness*, we have a good reason to extend the reference of "here" to the whole book.

If the above arguments are sound, we can then conclude that, in *Being and Nothingness*, Sartre did not endorse Detmer's distinction between ontological freedom and practical freedom. Accordingly, Detmer's resolution of the alleged inconsistency does not work.

Freedom versus Free Phantasy and Omnipotence

Having argued against Detmer's account to resolve the alleged inconsistency, I offer my own account in the following. Because my account is based on a new interpretation of freedom, let me start by clarifying the notion of freedom and other related notions.

In *Sartre's Two Ethics: From Authenticity to Integral Humanity*,[14] Thomas Anderson interpreted Sartre's freedom in *Being and Nothingness* as the spontaneity of consciousness,[15] the freedom of transcending one's circumstance* by whatever means,[16] which freedom in some cases is a freedom of dream and imagination.[17] Anderson said:

> In the final analysis, I believe that the freedom [in Sartre's *Being and Nothingness*] . . . is only a freedom of consciousness. . . . I believe that this freedom is ... not the concrete freedom of a situated human being. It may be true that the slave in chains can imagine and choose the not now existing goals of liberation or vacation at the seashore, and thereby in some sense transcend, negate, disengage himself, and escape from his present bondage—but only in thought, not in reality![18]

By claiming that the slave is free insofar as he can transcend his circumstance* by imagining the goal of a vacation at the seashore, Anderson interpreted Sartre's freedom as being in some cases *a freedom of dream and imagination, a free phantasy* that we can have at any time and place. But Sartre distinguished freedom from dream and wish in the chapter on freedom (EN, 562–63; BN, 621–22). And when Sartre introduced the distinction between freedom and dream, he says: "[W]e shall not say that a prisoner . . . is always free to long for release"(EN, 563–64; BN, 622). Now if Anderson is right—if free phantasies do count as freedom—then contrary to Sartre's claim, a prisoner is always free to long for release, insofar as he can always dream of release.

Freedom differs not only from free phantasy but also from omnipotence. "To be absolutely and totally free" should not be understood as having the ability to obtain whatever end we choose. Having the ability to obtain whatever end we choose entails encountering no obstacles—in Sartre's words "coefficient of adversity of things"[19]—in working toward the end chosen. However, according to Sartre, whatever end we choose, there are always obstacles to the obtaining of the end.[20] Suppose I choose to ride a bicycle to my school. When I ride uphill, the wind and the slope are obstacles. When I go downhill, the bad brake constitutes coefficient of adversity of things.

If freedom is neither free phantasy nor omnipotence, what exactly is it? According to Sartre, it is "the freedom of choice" (EN, 563; BN, 622). To understand this freedom of choice, we need to clarify the notion of choice.

Clarification of Choice

To spell out the meaning of "choice," let me first introduce the notion of "genuine project."

At many places in *Being and Nothingness* Sartre used the word 'project' in a very broad sense—to refer to any intentional conscious act (hereafter 'project*').[21] By "genuine project," I mean a goal-directed project* whose goal is both in principle *realizable* and *risky*[22] with respect to the agent in the circumstance*. Here note three things. First, if a project* is not a goal-directed consciousness, it is not a genuine project. Simple perceptions and imaginations by themselves are not genuine projects. Second, if a project* has a goal that is in principle unrealizable with respect to the agent in her particular circumstance*, it is *not* a genuine project. For a prisoner, the project* of freely walking out of the prison has an unrealizable goal (at least in some cases), and hence it is not a genuine project (in those cases).[23] For to a slave, the project* of obtaining the wealth and the standard of living of his master without fight is a dream, and hence not a genuine project.[24] Third, if a project* has a goal that is not risky, it is not a genuine project. For a prisoner, the project* of longing for release is not a genuine project, insofar as its goal is not risky (EN, 563–64; BN, 622).

This said, we are ready to define choice. *Choice is the formation of a genuine project plus a "commitment" to act on the project.* Here note three things. First, in forming a genuine project, I determine two things: I determine what I perceive, the circumstance* (e.g., I perceive a crag rather than a mirage or a magical object), and I determine the goal and the situation by interpreting the circumstance*, that is, predicating the perceived object or the state of affairs of certain value-bearing predicates (e.g., the crag is obstructive rather than helpful). Although *logically speaking*, the latter determination presupposes and is posterior to the former determination, *with respect to the being of consciousness*, these two determinations are done in one stroke, that is, *we are non-positionally aware (of) the two determinations simultaneously rather than one first and the other second*. Second, choice is more than the formation of a genuine project. Merely thinking of a genuine project without a "commitment" to act on the project is not a choice. Third, the "commitment" is not just a promise that I *will* carry out the project, but the initiation of the very project—the "commencement of realization" in Sartre's words (EN, 563;

BN, 622). To put it in another way, as soon as I have the commitment, I am acting on the project. Thus understood, choosing is tantamount to acting. And accordingly, Sartre saw no separation between intention and act, and avoided treating freedom as free phantasy (EN, 564; BN, 622).

This notion of choice differs from our ordinary notion of choice in three aspects. First, in ordinary language, a choice could be a choice of a project* that has an unrealizable or a non-risky goal. But a Sartrean choice is a choice of a genuine project, whose goal is both realizable and risky. Second, in ordinary language, we frequently say that we choose our being; for example, we choose to be an honest person, a kind person, etc. However, for Sartre a choice is in the first place *a choice of action*, not *a choice of being*. A Sartrean choice is concrete; it consists of a genuine project whose primary goal is an action to be performed, not a subjective state, a subjective quality, or a certain notion of the self to be possessed or realized (EN, 508–642; BN, 559–711). For example, if I choose to hate Peter, I have chosen the goal of performing certain actions toward Peter, rather than the goal of obtaining my hateful state or my quality of spitefulness.[25] Third, an indecision about doing X is a choice for Sartre (EN, 550–51, 561; BN, 607, 619), but not a choice in ordinary language. In ordinary language we draw a distinction between a decision not to do X and an indecision about doing X. Although a decision not to do X is a choice, an indecision about doing X—a suspended moment where no decision is reached—is not. For example, a decision not to take a job offer and an escape from decision by addicting oneself to alcohol may lead to the same result, but in ordinary language we say that the former, not the latter, is a choice. However, for Sartre, not only is a decision not to do X a choice, but also an indecision about doing X. Particularly, an indecision about doing X is a choice at a higher level—although the indecision is certainly not a decision about doing X, it is a decision at a higher level about *whether we should decide about doing X*. Thus, for Sartre we *must* choose in any circumstance, even when we are undecided about doing X.

Two Parts of Freedom

Having clarified the notion of choice, we now turn to freedom. Freedom—the freedom of choice—is for Sartre *the being of choice* (EN, 529–30; BN, 583). Because the being of choice is the non-positional consciousness (of) choice, *freedom is the non-positional consciousness (of) choice*. This non-positional consciousness contains two parts, the part about choosing[26] and the part about the project chosen.

The first part (the part about the choosing) includes the non-positional consciousness that *I am autonomous to form and to commit myself to act on the project chosen among a range of genuine projects*. The autonomy here is a combination of *the autonomy of my determining what I perceive, the autonomy of my predicating the perceived object or state of affairs*, and *the autonomy of committing myself to act on the chosen project*. This autonomy is "absolute," in the sense that the autonomy is total and is not relative to the circumstance, time, and place. Suppose I stop in front of a crag (EN, 562; BN, 620). When I form and commit myself to act on a genuine project of displacing the crag, I have the non-positional consciousness that I don't have to form and to commit myself to act on the project—I could have formed and committed myself to act on another genuine project, for example, a genuine project of climbing upon the crag to see the landscape. Moreover, the autonomy manifested in the non-positional consciousness is *absolute*, in the sense that the autonomy is total and is not relative to the circumstance, time, and place. It is total, because I alone decide whether to form and to commit myself to act on the project of displacing the crag. It is not relative to the circumstance, time, and place, because no matter when, where, and in what circumstance, as far as I am choosing, I am autonomous to form and to commit myself to act on a genuine project.

The second part (the part about the project chosen) includes the non-positional consciousnesses that the project chosen is a genuine project and that I am not autonomous to determine whether the project chosen is a genuine project. Another way to put the latter is this: Although we have autonomy to determine *which* project to form and to commit ourselves to act on among a range of genuine projects, we don't have autonomy in determining *the range of genuine projects* from which we choose. In forming and committing myself to act on the project of displacing the crag, although I decide whether to form and to commit myself to act on the project, I cannot make displacing the crag *not to be* a genuine project, *not to be* a potential object for our choice. Moreover, although I can form and commit myself to act on any genuine project, I cannot make anything a genuine project. To determine whether something is a genuine project, I have to consider *the circumstance* and use this criterion: X is a genuine project if and only if X is a goal-directed project* whose goal is in principle realizable and risky under a possible circumstance*—a possible disclosure of the circumstance in physical terms. In the crag example, it is a genuine project to climb upon the crag to see the landscape, but it is not a genuine project to convert the crag to a person. In the prisoner example, it is a genuine project to have a fast for several days, but it is not a genuine project to go shopping. In the master/slave example, it is a genuine project for the slave to beat the master, but it is not a genuine project for the slave to have a luxurious life without fight. In sum, from these examples we see that the circumstance plays a role in determining whether something is a genuine project. Hence, the second part of non-positional consciousness (of) choice manifests a qualification by the circumstance, insofar as one quality of the genuine projects formed and acted on—the quality of being a genuine project—is in part[27] determined by the circumstance.

Given the division of the two parts of freedom (the non-positional consciousness [of] choice), we can resolve the alleged inconsistency. When Sartre claimed that we are "absolutely free," "totally free," "wholly and forever free," and "condemned to be free," he was talking about the absolute autonomy in *the first part of freedom*. When Sartre said that our freedom is limited, he was talking about the qualification in *the second part of freedom*. Understood in this way, the sentences "freedom is absolute" and "freedom is limited" are neither contradictions nor contraries. And there is indeed *no* inconsistency between Sartre's views that we are absolutely free and that our freedom is limited: Our freedom is at the same time absolute (the autonomy of choice is absolute) and limited (our project's being a legitimate object of choice is qualified by the circumstance).

Having resolved the alleged inconsistency, let's further explore the characteristics of freedom.

One important characteristic of freedom is that it is *individualistic*. Whenever I choose, the circumstance and my facticity determine whether something is a genuine project. Having a vacation is a genuine project for a person having spare time and money, but not a genuine project for a person in prison. Participating in a future Olympic soccer game is a genuine project for a distinguished soccer player, but not a genuine project for a person who has lost a leg in an accident. Because a state description of the circumstance and my facticity is unique, the pool of genuine projects available to me in a given circumstance is unique. Hence, freedom is individualistic, insofar as it is forming and committing oneself to act on a genuine project *among a unique pool of genuine projects*.

Freedom is not only individualistic, but also *non-measurable*. We know that freedom is forming and committing oneself to act on a genuine project among a pool of genuine projects. Now, it is obvious that the act of forming and committing oneself to act on a project is not measurable. For it makes no sense to talk about *a bit of* forming, *a lot of* forming, and so on.

Because freedom is non-measurable, it is incomparable.[28] We can compare two freedoms only if they can be measured in the same terms. But freedoms cannot be measured. Hence, they cannot be compared. When Sartre said that the slave is as free as the master, he was not suggesting that the slave's freedom has *the same quantity* as the master's; rather, he meant that (1) both the slave and the master are free and (2) their freedoms cannot be measured and compared.[29]

Freedom, Internal Negation, and the Ontological Proof

In the foregoing, I have offered my interpretation of freedom and discussed some characteristics of freedom. In this section, I argue that my interpretation sheds light on two important notions in Sartre's ontology, "internal negation" and "the ontological proof."

"Internal negation" is an important notion in Sartre's ontology: It plays a central role in accounting for the relation "between" the for-itself and the in-itself, the relation between the for-itself and its intentional object, and the relation between the for-itself and the other for-itselfs.

As I said in chapter 2, "internal negation" can be understood as a bridge to the in-itself in the very being of the for-itself, insofar as it is the ontological relation that the for-itself bears to the in-itself, through which relation the for-itself points toward the in-itself (EN, 223; BN, 243). It constitutes the very being of the for-itself (EN, 224; BN, 243–44); i.e., we are non-positionally aware (of) the internal negation.

The internal negation (we are non-positionally aware [of]) cannot have the form of an ordinary denial. It cannot have the form of "X's (e.g., the for-itself's) not being Y (e.g., the in-itself)." For if it does, it is not different from a counterpart of the external negation at the non-positional side. It cannot have the form "not being X" either. For if X is the in-itself (i.e., if the internal negation is the denial of the in-itself), we must be aware (of) the in-itself at the non-positional side. But then the in-itself is *a part of the being of consciousness* rather than *something to which consciousness bears an ontological relation.* If X is not the in-itself, what else can X be? It cannot be consciousness itself. For if it is, either we have to substantialize consciousness or we will have to admit that consciousness is unintelligible—it is the denial of the denial of the denial of . . . .

If the internal negation is not an ordinary denial, what exactly is it? To answer this question, let's look closely at the above account of freedom.

According to the above account, freedom has two parts. One part includes the non-positional consciousness that I am autonomous to form and to commit myself to act on the project chosen among a range of genuine objects, and the other part includes the non-positional consciousness that I am not autonomous to determine whether the project chosen is a genuine project. The two non-positional consciousnesses (in two parts of freedom) are not really contradictory, since my having autonomy in forming and committing myself to act on the project chosen among a range of genuine projects is compatible with my not having autonomy in determining the range of genuine projects. Nevertheless, they (the two non-positional consciousnesses) constitute an "intrinsic" contrast, insofar as one has the form "I am autonomous . . ." and the other has the form "I am not autonomous . . . ."[30] The contrast between them is "intrinsic," because neither of them can be grasped as what it is without its contrasting with the other. Consider the non-positional consciousness that I am autonomous to form and to commit myself to act on the project chosen among a range of genuine projects. It can be grasped as "I am autonomous . . ." *only if there is a co-present non-positional consciousness in the form "I am not autonomous . . ." from which (non-positional consciousness) it is distinguished.* For if there is no such non-positional consciousness, 'autonomy' will become a meaningless word. Moreover, the only non-positional consciousness in freedom that has the form "I am not autonomous . . ." is the non-positional consciousness that I am not autonomous to determine whether the project chosen is a genuine project. Thus, the non-positional consciousness that I am autonomous to form and to commit myself to act on the project chosen among a range of genuine projects can be grasped as what it is only through its contrasting with the non-positional consciousness that I am not autonomous to determine whether the project chosen is a genuine project. Using similar reasons, we can show that the non-positional consciousness that I am not autonomous to determine whether the project chosen is a genuine project can be grasped as what it is only through its contrasting with the non-positional consciousness that I am autonomous to form and to commit myself to act on the project chosen among a range of genuine projects. In sum, the contrast between the two non-positional consciousnesses is intrinsic to their being grasped as what they are.

The internal negation—in the case of freedom—can be understood in terms of the intrinsic contrast between the two non-positional consciousnesses (of) freedom. The intrinsic contrast points to a *negation,* because of the following reason: By observing the non-positional consciousness that I am autonomous to form and to commit myself to act on the project chosen among a range of genuine projects, we are inclined to equate consciousness with autonomy in general. However, this equation is negated when we observe the non-positional consciousness that I am not autonomous to determine whether the project chosen is a genuine project. The intrinsic contrast is *internal*, because (1) the contrast is found in the being of freedom and (2) it is intrinsic in the sense discussed before.

Not only does my account of freedom help explain internal negation in the case of freedom, but also, it can be used to explain internal negation in general. For those who equate consciousness with freedom,[31] the explanation above is simply for internal negation in general. For those who think there are other sorts of consciousness besides freedom, the explanation above can be extended to cover other sorts of consciousness. For example, take perceptual consciousness in general.[32] In those consciousnesses, the internal negation can be understood in terms of the intrinsic contrast between the two non-positional consciousnesses (of) perceiving. On the one hand, I am non-positionally aware that I don't have to see in the way that I actually see (e.g., in seeing a rabbit I could have seen a rabbit stage, undetached rabbit parts, etc.). In other words, I am autonomous to determine the way to see among a range of possible ways of seeing. On the other hand, I am non-positionally aware that I cannot see in any way that I want to see (e.g., in seeing a rabbit I cannot see a pig if I keep our ordinary usage of "pig"). In other words, I am not autonomous to determine the range of possible ways of seeing. This said, I hasten to add that the autonomy in perceptual consciousness in general is weaker than that in freedom. Whereas in perceptual consciousness in general we decide only what we see (e.g., whether we see a crag), in freedom we decide not only what we see but also the value-bearing predicates of what we see (e.g., whether the crag is obstructive).

As we know, Sartre claimed that internal negation can be understood as a bridge to the in-itself. How do we account for that feature in our explanation?

To answer this question, let's consider the non-positional consciousness that I am not autonomous to determine whether the project chosen is a genuine project. How should we understand this non-positional consciousness? If it is not up to me to decide whether something is a genuine project, doesn't it mean that there is something else that is responsible for determining the range of genuine projects, given that I do choose from a range of genuine projects? Now, this something else—the circumstance and my facticity—is the in-itself.

Note that in order for the above understanding of the non-positional consciousness to be possible, the non-positional consciousness must be grasped as that I am not autonomous to determine whether the project chosen is a genuine project. But the non-positional consciousness can be grasped as this only through my contrasting it with the non-positional consciousness that I am autonomous to form and to commit myself to act on the project chosen among a range of genuine projects (as I discussed in the previous section). Thus, the contrast between the two non-positional consciousnesses is an essential element that helps us reach the in-itself. In this sense, the contrast between the two non-positional consciousnesses, that is, my explanation of internal negation in the case of freedom, can be understood as a bridge to the in-itself. Using the similar line of reasoning, we can show that the contrast between the two non-positional consciousnesses in perceptual consciousness in general can be understood as a bridge to the in-itself.

The above outlines a way to get to the in-itself in the very being of consciousness, which I suggest is one way "the ontological proof" might go. According to Sartre, in the *Introduction* to *Being and Nothingness*, the ontological proof is this: Non-positional consciousness is "a revealing intuition," and that a revealing intuition "implies something revealed" (the in-itself) (EN, 29; BN, 23). Why is non-positional consciousness a *revealing intuition*?

It is not hard to answer this question using our account of freedom. With respect to the relation between freedom and its intentional object—the (interpreted) situation—(the non-positional consciousness [of]) freedom is best understood as a *revealing intuition* because of the two contrasting non-positional consciousnesses (of) freedom. It is not appropriate to understand freedom as a *creation* of the situation because it includes the non-positional consciousness that I am not autonomous to determine whether the project chosen is a genuine project[33]. It is not appropriate either to understand freedom as a *report* of the situation, because it includes the non-positional consciousness that I am autonomous to form and to commit myself to act on the project chosen among a range of genuine projects. Using similar reasoning, we can show that (the non-positional consciousness [of]) perceptual consciousness in general is best understood as a revealing intuition.

Detmer's Objection Answered

Finally, let me address an objection that Detmer raised to my interpretation of freedom. The objection runs as follows: At many places, Sartre claimed that the slave is not as free as the master and that a free being such as a slave is in need of liberation. If my account is right—particularly if freedom is non-measurable—how can we make sense of the above claims?

To support the thesis that, at many places Sartre claimed that the slave is not as free as the master and that a free being such as a slave is in need of liberation, Detmer cited three passages:

> But, say the Marxists, if you teach man that he *is* free, you betray him; for he no longer needs to *become* free; can you conceive of a man free from birth who demands to be liberated? To this I reply that if man is not originally free, but determined once and for all, we cannot even conceive what his liberation might be.[34]

> It is not true that a free man cannot hope to be liberated. For he is not free and bound in respect to the same thing.[35]

> But what would it mean to liberate a man whose actions were determined? If man were not free, it would not be worth moving a finger for him.[36]

I agree that in the above passages, Sartre did suggest that a free being might still need liberation. However, none of these passages are from *Being and Nothingness*: The first two are from "Materialism and Revolution," which was published in 1949[37] (six years after the publication of *Being and Nothingness*), and the last one is from an interview in 1946 (three years after the publication of *Being and Nothingness*). Moreover, nowhere in *Being and Nothingness* did Sartre claim or hint that the slave is not as free as the master. Rather, he made this claim (that the slave is not as free as the master) only in his later works, for example, in "Materialism and Revolution."[38] Thus, Detmer established only that Sartre held the claims that the slave is not as free as the master and that a free being such as a slave is in need of liberation in his post-*Being and Nothingness* works, but not that Sartre held these claims in *Being and Nothingness*.

This said, we see that Detmer's objection rests on an assumption that Sartre had a univocal theory of freedom in his early philosophy—in particular he did not change or enrich the notion of freedom after *Being and Nothingness*. However, this assumption might not be true, because (1) there is extensive textual evidence in Sartre's later works—including those mentioned above—that suggests a change or enrichment of Sartre's views about freedom, and (2) it is not obvious that this assumption has theoretical advantages (Detmer did not give any).[39] Because Detmer's objection rests on a problematic assumption, it is not clear that the objection works.

Conclusion

In this chapter, I have offered an interpretation of Sartre's freedom in *Being and Nothingness*, and I have argued that this interpretation sheds light on two important notions in Sartre's ontology, "internal negation" and "the ontological proof." Through dividing freedom—the non-positional consciousness (of) choice—into two parts, I have developed an account that I argue can accommodate both Sartre's claim that our freedom is absolute and his claim that our freedom is limited. As a result, I conclude that there is indeed no inconsistency in Sartre's views about freedom in *Being and Nothingness*: His claim that our freedom is absolute is compatible with his claim that our freedom is limited.

Notes

1. I take "circumstance" as the surrounding in-itself. I use 'circumstance*' to refer to the surrounding state of affairs— the disclosure of circumstance in *physical* terms. Note that for Sartre "situation" is neither circumstance nor circumstance*, because for Sartre a "situation" is a circumstance* interpreted in the light of our freely chosen end (EN, 562–63; BN, 620–21).

2. Dagfinn Føllesdal, "Sartre on Freedom," in *The Philosophy of Jean-Paul Sartre*, ed. Paul Arthur Schilpp (La Salle, Ill.: Open Court, 1981), 392–407.

3. Riseiri Frondizi, "Sartre's Early Ethics: A Critique," in Schilpp, *The Philosophy of Jean-Paul Sartre*, 383–88.

4. Walter Kaufmann, *Without Guilt and Justice* (New York: Delta, 1973), 144.

5. Hubert Marcuse, "Sartre's Existentialism" in his *Studies in Critical Philosophy* (Boston: Beacon Press, 1973), 172–77.

6. Mary Warnock, *The Philosophy of Jean-Paul Sartre* (New York: Barnes & Noble, 1967), 112.

7. David Detmer, *Freedom as a Value: A Critique of the Ethical Theory of Jean-Paul Sartre* (La Salle, Ill.: Open Court, 1986).

8. Detmer, *Freedom as a Value*, 60.

9. Detmer, *Freedom as a Value*, 64–65.

10. Practical freedom is measured in terms of degrees. At one extreme, where there is the maximum degree of practical freedom, practical freedom is tantamount to omnipotence.

11. According to Detmer, consciousness is ontologically free in the sense that "it is *not* its situation—that, through its nihilating behaviors, it can separate itself from all that is external to it, and from whatever might attempt to ensnare or enslave it, and, in so doing, disentangle itself from the chain of causal determinism" (Detmer, *Freedom as a Value*, 63–64). Detmer did not specify the exact scope of the nihilating behaviors used to transcend the circumstance* ("situation" in Detmer's words), but he claimed that mere inner acts such as wishful thinkings, dreams, and imaginations do not count as the nihilating behaviors (Detmer, *Freedom as a Value*, 69–70).

12. Detmer, *Freedom as a Value*, 62–69.

13. Note that there is a difference between the claim that Sartre *did not consider* practical freedom in *Being and Nothingness* and the claim that Sartre *rejected* practical freedom in *Being and Nothingness*. In the paper, I hold the former claim, but I do not hold the latter. I am grateful to David Detmer for pointing out this subtle difference.

14. Thomas Anderson, *Sartre's Two Ethics: From Authenticity to Integral Humanity* (La Salle, Ill.: Open Court, 1993).

15. "[T]he early Sartre does identity it [freedom] with total [un]conditioned (therefore, free) spontaneity" (Anderson, *Sartre's Two Ethics*, 24, note 29).

16. Anderson, *Sartre's Two Ethics*, 19, 24.

17. Note the difference between Anderson's freedom and Detmer's ontological freedom. Although they are both freedoms of transcending the circumstance*, Anderson's freedom is in some cases a freedom of transcending the circumstance* *in dream and imagination*, whereas Detmer's ontological freedom is not.

18. Anderson, *Sartre's Two Ethics*, 24.

19. I disagree with Detmer on his interpretation of the coefficient of adversity of things. According to Detmer, the coefficient of adversity of things is what limits the range of our possible projects: "[I]t is plain that the coefficient of adversity of the crag also limits the range of projects that I might choose to undertake with respect to it. Because I cannot regard the crag as a poached egg which is singing a song, I can undertake neither the project of putting it on the toast and eating it for breakfast, nor that of joining its singing while accompanying it on guitar" (Detmer, *Freedom as a Value*, 46). But this is not what Sartre meant by "the coefficient of adversity of things." For Sartre it means the resistance of an object (or a state of affairs) *in a particular project*, the meaning of an object (or a state of affairs) for the subject in the context of the chosen project, rather than what limits the range of possible projects. Sartre says: "In particular the coefficient of adversity in things can not [cannot] be an argument against our freedom, for it is *by us*—i.e., by the preliminary posting of an end—that this coefficient of adversity arises. A particular

crag, which manifests a profound resistance if I wish to displace it, will be on the contrary a valuable aid if I want to climb upon it in order to look over the countryside. In itself—if one can even imagine what the crag can be in itself—it is neutral; that is, it waits to be illuminated by an end in order to manifest itself as adverse or helpful" (EN, 562; BN, 620).

20. Not only is freedom not the lack of the coefficient of adversity of things[40] (EN, 561–62; BN, 619–20), but it arises only in the context where the coefficient of adversity of things is present—indeed it causes the coefficient of adversity of things to appear in the world (EN, 562; BN, 620).

21. However, occasionally Sartre used 'project' in the sense of a genuine project. E.g., see EN, 635; BN, 703.

22. When I say the goal of a project is *risky*, I mean that there are obstacles to the realization of the goal; in other words, there is a *real* possibility that the goal cannot be successfully achieved.

23. "Thus we shall not say that a prisoner is always free to go out of prison, which would be absurd" (EN, 563; BN, 622).

24. "Of course the slave will not be able to obtain the wealth and the standard of living of his master; but these are not the objects of his *projects*; he can only dream of the possession of these treasures" (EN, 635; BN, 703).

25. For a detailed discussion, see TL, 37–44; TE, 54–60.

26. When Sartre said that freedom is "the autonomy of choice" (EN, 563; BN, 622), he was referring to this part of freedom.

27. "In part" because my facticity—the disclosure of the in-itself as facts about myself—also plays a role here.

28. Being non-measurable and incomparable, freedom does not meet a common expectation that we rank desirability of different circumstances* in terms of the quantities of the freedoms we have in the circumstances*. In other words, if freedom is non-measurable and incomparable, then we have no need to change any circumstance* to increase our freedom. It is this problem, I think, that motivated Sartre to revise his notion of freedom later on.

29. "[T]he situation of the slave *can not* [*cannot*] *be compared* with that of the master. Each of them in fact takes on its meaning only for the for-itself in situation and in terms of the free choice of its ends" (EN, 635; BN, 703).

30. To put it in another way, we find in one an instantiation of the predicate "my being autonomous in doing . . ." and we find in the other an instantiation of the complementary predicate "my not being autonomous in doing . . . ."

31. All commentators agree that every consciousness is "free" in the sense of being spontaneous. However, not all agree that every consciousness is the (goal-directed) freedom. According to my account of freedom, freedom is a proper subset of consciousness.

32. Of course, there are other sorts of consciousness, e.g., imagination, conception. However, in *Being and Nothingness*, Sartre was primarily interested in perceptual consciousness.

33. In other words, it is not true that I can have any situation I want.

34. Jean-Paul Sartre, "Materialism and Revolution," in his *Literary and Philosophical Essays*, trans. by Annette Michelson (New York: Coller, 1962), 244.

35. Sartre, "Materialism and Revolution," 245.

36. Jean-Paul Sartre, interview with Jean Duché, quoted in Dagfinn Føllesdal, "Sartre on Freedom," 404–5.

37. This article was originally published as "Matérialisme et révolution," in his *Situations* III (Paris: Gallimard, 1949).

38. "This inner freedom is a pure idealist hoax. . . . If Epictetus, in chains, does not rebel, it is because he feels free, because he enjoys his freedom. On that basis, one state is as good as another, the slave's situation is as good as the master's; why should anyone want to change it? . . . What remains for the slave are abstract thoughts and empty intentions, under the name of metaphysical freedom" (Sartre, "Materialism and Revolution," 237).

39. I think that Sartre changed or at least enriched his notion of freedom after *Being and Nothingness*. It is not the right place to discuss Sartre's later views about freedom. But let me point out here that Sartre's later freedoms are measurable qualities of substance rather than the being of consciousness—they include Detmer's practical freedom and the freedom of choosing situations (with respect to which the master is more free than the slave, because the master can have a situation similar to the one the slave faces by choosing to be a slave, whereas the slave cannot have a situation similar to the one the master faces insofar as the slave cannot choose to be a master without much fight).

Chapter Four

Bad Faith in Sartre's *Being and Nothingness*

Introduction

It is widely recognized that Sartre's interest in discussing bad faith in *Being and Nothingness* was mainly ontologically oriented. However, many commentators, most notably Ronald Santoni in his recent book, *Bad Faith, Good Faith, and Authenticity in Sartre's Early Philosophy*, held that in Sartre's early works, especially in *Being and Nothingness*, the ontological characteristics of bad faith and the contrast between good faith and bad faith have non-trivial ethical implications. For, according to them, bad faith is fundamentally an ontological attitude of fleeing one's freedom and responsibility, whereas good faith is an attitude of accepting one's freedom and responsibility.[1] This interpretation is attractive at first sight, because it provides a basis for a unified account of bad faith in Sartre's early philosophy, especially how the ontological characteristics of bad faith as stated in *Being and Nothingness* can be tightly and significantly linked with the ethical treatment of bad faith in *Notebooks for an Ethics*. Nevertheless, a careful examination of Sartre's views on bad faith in *Being and Nothingness* will reveal that this interpretation is ultimately false. It is the purpose of this chapter to take on that task. In what follows, I shall pursue a detailed study of the conditions of the possibility of bad faith in several stages of increasing depth, in order to reveal completely the ontological structures of bad faith. On the basis of that, I shall argue that in *Being and Nothingness* (1) the ontological characteristics of bad faith have only *trivial* ethical implication, and (2) the contrast between good faith and bad faith does not have any *salient* ethical implication, and it *was not* intended by Sartre as a contrast between the ontological attitudes of accepting or fleeing one's freedom and responsibility.

Is Bad Faith Possible as an Ontological Project?

A quick yet commonly held criticism of Sartre's theory of bad faith is that the project of bad faith[2] is ontologically impossible,[3] since (1) lying to oneself is ontologically impossible, given the translucency of consciousness; and (2) Sartre introduced bad faith as a lie to oneself at the beginning of his chapter on bad faith (EN, 86; BN, 87). According to this criticism, "(2)" is a given, and "(1)" follows directly from the fact that in any project of lying to ourselves—a project in which we hide a truth from ourselves and/or present an untruth to ourselves as the truth—we must be non-positionally aware (of) the truth and our affecting ourselves with the deceitful project. Is this criticism tenable?

Occasionally, people accept "(1)" simply on the ground that they regard lying to oneself as a special case of ordinary lying in general.[4] Now certainly "(1)" would be right if lying to oneself were a special case of lying in general. But Sartre clearly distinguished lying to oneself from lying in general at several places (EN, 86, 87, 108; BN, 87, 89, 112).[5]

In other cases, people frequently use the two difficulties that Sartre mentioned in *Section I* of the chapter on bad faith as the crucial evidence to support "(1),"[6] and some even go on to claim that Sartre *intended* to use the two difficulties to disprove, or at least cast doubt on, the ontological possibility of bad faith. However, it seems to me that both moves are just false, which I shall show in the following.

The two difficulties that Sartre mentioned in the text are these: (a) We know that in bad faith the deceiver and the deceived are one, and the agent of bad faith both "knows" and conceals the truth in a single consciousness. But then how can the lie subsist in the project of bad faith (EN, 88; BN, 89)? (b) Given that consciousness is translucent, "[t]hat which affects itself with bad faith must be conscious (of) its bad faith since the being of consciousness is consciousness of being" (EN, 88; BN, 89). But then the whole project of bad faith is annihilated: "the lie falls back and collapses beneath my look; it is ruined *from behind* by the very consciousness of lying to myself which pitilessly constitutes itself well within my project as its very condition" (EN, 88; BN, 89). In order to determine whether "(a)" or "(b)" supports "(1)," let us consider them respectively.

First, let us look at "(b)." All "(b)" says is that bad faith is an evanescent phenomenon with a so-called metastable structure (EN, 88; BN, 89–

90). It clearly does not imply "(1)," for how can the evanescent character of bad faith, however undesirable it may appear to some people, be the ground that the project of bad faith is ontologically impossible, that is, bad faith cannot even be *attempted*?

Next, let us consider "(a)." Part of what "(a)" says is that in the project of bad faith one "knows" and conceals the truth at the same time. On the surface this might seem to be impossible, for if we literally know the truth, how can we conceal, or even try to conceal, the truth from ourselves at the same time? But notice that what Sartre meant here by "knowing the truth" is really the non-positional awareness (of) the truth, not, properly speaking, the knowledge* of the truth. Moreover, when we try to conceal the truth, we simply do not try to conceal it on the non-positional side; instead, we try to keep the truth from being *an object of positional consciousness*. On the face of it, there seems to be no reason why we cannot have this kind of mental act. No doubt, given the fact that we are non-positionally aware (of) the truth that we are trying to conceal, in bad faith we cannot completely succeed in deceiving ourselves. However, *it is one thing to say that the project of bad faith cannot be completely successful, and it is quite another thing to say that the project of bad faith is ontologically impossible.*

Hence, when properly understood, neither "(a)" nor "(b)" provides support for "(1)." Moreover, for Sartre the existence of projects of bad faith is just a *brute fact*, and thus any doubt concerning the ontological possibility of bad faith is totally wrong-headed at the beginning. When Sartre asked how the lie can subsist in bad faith, he was not questioning the ontological possibility of bad faith. Rather, he was questioning the legitimacy of trying to understand bad faith in terms of the model of lying in general, and he presupposed that bad faith is in fact possible. It is true that for Sartre "(a)" and "(b)" are genuine difficulties; however, they are not difficulties *concerning the existence of bad faith*, but difficulties *concerning our understanding of bad faith*. This is clear when we see that Sartre, immediately after presenting "(a)" and "(b)," said that "[o]ur embarrassment then appears extreme since we can neither reject nor comprehend bad faith" (EN, 88; BN, 90).

Under this line of reading, by presenting "(a)" and "(b)," and thereupon showing that consciousness in bad faith involves much more subtle kinds of behavior than lying in general, Sartre's aim was to stimulate a comprehensive analysis of bad faith, in addition to and independent of our understanding of lying in general. And the way that we should carry out the analysis of bad faith, Sartre suggested, is to question the conditions of the possibility of bad faith. This questioning starts from a presentation of the various patterns of behavior that bad faith can take.

After distinguishing bad faith from lying in general, and clarifying Sartre's strategy underlying a series of interrogations that he brought forward under the initial approximation of bad faith in terms of lying in general, we are now ready to investigate the conditions of the possibility of bad faith. Let us start with the notorious waiter example.

The First Presupposition of Bad Faith

In spite of some exceptions,[7] the waiter example is commonly taken as one that was *used* by Sartre to illustrate the patterns of bad faith, and the reason for this is simply that the waiter example occurs in the section entitled "Patterns of Bad Faith." However, Sartre himself *never said* that the waiter in the example is in bad faith, while in other major examples in that section, that is, the young woman example, the homosexual and his critic example, the evil man example, and the coward example (EN, 94–95, 103–5, 105, 107; BN, 96–98, 107–9, 109, 111), he explicitly said they are. Certainly this is not a sufficient reason to reject the claim that the waiter example was introduced to illustrate the patterns of bad faith, but neither is it sufficient to accept the claim on the meager basis that the waiter example is contained in the section entitled "Patterns of Bad Faith."

The claim I would like to establish firmly is that the waiter example *was not* given in the text *for the purpose of illustrating* the patterns of bad faith, although I leave it open whether or not the waiter in fact is or has to be in bad faith in the example.[8] To justify this claim, we need to look closely at the context of the waiter example.

The general aim of the section "Patterns of Bad Faith" is to give an initial approach to the conditions of the possibility of bad faith, and to reply to the question "What must be the being of man if he is to be capable of bad faith" (EN, 94; BN, 96)? Sartre started this section with the famous example of the young woman. And after describing the various kinds of behavior that the woman adopts in sustaining bad faith, Sartre concluded that the woman uses distorted understandings of two distinctions, the transcendence/facticity distinction and the being-for-itself/being-for-others distinction, to maintain herself in bad faith (EN, 95–96, 97; BN, 97–99, 100). But if this is the case, Sartre asked, "what exactly is necessary in order for these concepts of disintegration to be able to receive even a pretence of existence, in order for them to be able to appear for an instant to consciousness, even in a process of evanescence" (EN, 97–98; BN, 100)? Using this question as a guiding thread, Sartre hoped to lead us directly into the instantaneous nucleus of consciousness and to discover the relation between consciousness and the "in-itself" (what I call the "in-itself*")[9] (that consciousness tries to be) in the project of "making to be the in-itself*."[10]

Sartre's strategy was to begin with a *reductio* argument, in which he argued that if man were just what he is, sincerity would become the being of rather than the value for human beings, which contradicts the fact that sincerity is a value for human beings (EN, 98; BN, 101). Then, to explain the non-coincidence between consciousness and what it is, and to illustrate the relation between consciousness and the in-itself* in the project of "making to be the in-itself*," Sartre introduced the waiter example and the sadness example. In particular, the waiter example was given to illustrate the relation between consciousness and the in-itself* in the project of "making to be social positions" (EN, 100; BN, 103), and the sadness example was given to illustrate the relation between consciousness and the in-itself* in the project of "making to be conscious states" (EN, 100–1; BN, 103–4). And then, having explicated the structure of consciousness in the project of "making to be the in-itself*," Sartre went on to show us how this very structure facilitates the various behaviors of bad faith, in which he discussed several instances of "sincerity" (e.g., the homosexual's critic, the evil man, etc.) and the homosexual example and the coward example (EN, 102–7; BN, 105–11). Under this line of reading, it seems clear that the waiter example was introduced solely for the purpose of illustrating the general structure of consciousness in the project of "making to be the in-itself*"—the relation between consciousness and the in-itself* (that consciousness tries to be), but not for the purpose of illustrating the patterns of bad faith.

Now, if the waiter example was introduced to illustrate the relation between consciousness and the in-itself* in the project of "making to be the in-itself*," what then is the relation? A careful consideration of the waiter example and the sadness example will lead to the following observations:

The project of "making to be the in-itself*" presupposes that consciousness is distanced from the in-itself*. In order to make itself to be the in-itself*, consciousness must be separated from the in-itself*; otherwise the in-itself* would become the being of rather than the goal for consciousness. If I can be a waiter or become sad, that is only because I am not the person or the state that I try to be.

Although consciousness always tries to make itself to be the in-itself*,
it can never completely succeed in turning itself into the in-itself*. First,
consciousness has no "inertia," and it cannot hold on to its realization of
the in-itself* (that it created before) without continuously recreating it—in
the project of "making to be the in-itself*," as soon as the "making" act
ceases, the realization of the in-itself* also ceases to be.[11] Second, in the
"making" project, consciousness is always non-positionally aware (of) its
"making" act, and by means of this non-positional awareness, it "knows"
that it is not the in-itself* that it makes itself to be.[12]

Although consciousness cannot successfully turn itself into the in-
itself*, through the "making" act, consciousness does realize the in-itself*
in a sense, if we limit our considerations to the exhibited behaviors. If I
make myself to be a waiter, during the "making" project, I am nothing other
than the collection of my behaviors, that is, the precise and quick movement, the inflexible stiff walk, the eagerness for the order, etc., which
constitutes the social position "waiter" (EN, 98; BN, 101). However, I am
a waiter not as being in-itself*, but "in the mode of being what I am not"
(EN, 100; BN, 103), since the in-itself* of the waiter and my non-positional
awareness (of) being a waiter have different modalities, and it totally
depends on me whether to sustain myself as being the waiter or not.

To summarize the above, Sartre used his famous doctrine that
"consciousness is not what it is and is what it is not." To emphasize the
(qualified) realization of the in-itself* in the "making" project, we may say
that consciousness is what it is not (EN, 100; BN, 103), and to emphasize
the making act that brings forth the realization of the in-itself*, the way that
"making sustains being," we may say that consciousness is not what it is
(EN, 102; BN, 105), although these two clauses really should not be taken
separately in describing the relation between consciousness and the in-
itself* in the project of "making to be the in-itself*."[13]

As I mentioned earlier, the paradoxical doctrine that consciousness is
not what it is and is what it is not does not have a univocal sense in *Being
and Nothingness*. As one might expect, when Sartre went deeper and
deeper into his investigations, the content of this doctrine became richer
and richer. In the *Introduction* to *Being and Nothingness*, we can see a
preliminary elucidation of this doctrine, that from the general standpoint of
intentionality, "consciousness is born *supported* by a being which is not
itself" (EN, 28; BN, 23). Later on, when Sartre discussed the vertigo
example and the gambler example (EN, 67–69, 69–71; BN, 66–69, 69–70),
he enriched the meaning of the doctrine by claiming that consciousness is

its future (what it is not yet) and is not its past (what it was). Furthermore, in *section II* of the chapter on bad faith, as we have seen in the above, the doctrine was used to describe the relation between consciousness and the in-itself* (that consciousness tries to be) in the instantaneous nucleus of consciousness. And still more, in *section III* of that chapter, we shall see another sense of the doctrine which I will discuss later.

The third sense of the paradoxical doctrine, that consciousness both is and is not the in-itself* in the project of "making to be the in-itself*," is far from being trivial. Indeed, it serves as a justificatory ground for agents of bad faith to perform various kinds of distortions: In the young woman example, the homosexual example, and the coward example, we see that it is the comprehension of the contradictory structure of consciousness that enables people in bad faith to form deceitful concepts.[14] In the instances of "sincerity"[15] (e.g., the critic of the homosexual, the evil man, etc.), by actively engaging themselves with the "sincerity" project—the project of being what one is (a species of the project of "making to be the in-itself*"), the agents of bad faith try to escape from what they are by appealing to the contradictory relation between consciousness and the in-itself* in the very project.[16]

So far we have spelled out *a* condition of the possibility of bad faith, that in every project of "making to be the in-itself*," consciousness is what it is not and is not what it is. But is it the *only* condition that is presupposed by bad faith? I do not think so. It is true that this structure of consciousness does play a significant role in the *formations* of various sorts of distortions in bad faith, but we have not yet touched the more general *question—how are distortions as a whole, or rather, the category of distortions in bad faith, possible?* So now, we must ask ourselves the following questions: What is the nature of the category of distortions in bad faith? And how is that possible?[17] To answer them, we need to proceed from the notion of "mere belief."

The Second Presupposition of Bad Faith

A mere belief, as Sartre claimed, is a belief supported by only insufficient evidence or no evidence at all, a belief having the character of "adherence of being to its object when the object is not given or is given indistinctly" (EN, 108; BN, 112), in contrast to a knowing belief, which is completely fulfilled by the evidence. In other words, if we try to believe something without having (sufficient) evidence, if we appeal to faith rather than evidence to sustain the belief, the belief we have is a mere belief. Now, if bad faith is mere belief,[18] it does not seem to be very hard to explain the characteristic of distortions in bad faith and its condition of possibility, because the characteristic of a mere belief and its possibility are relatively straightforward and clear.

Nevertheless, equating bad faith with mere belief without qualification is too good to be true. There are two reasons. First, bad faith differs from a mere belief *simpliciter* in the sense that, in bad faith, we always require *some* evidence,[19] and we determine the nature of the evidence to be "*non-persuasive* evidence" (EN, 109; BN, 113). Second, and more important, bad faith differs from a mere belief *simpliciter* in the structure and the goal of the believing project: Unlike a mere belief *simpliciter*, the goal of bad faith is to produce what might be called "*quasi-beliefs*," the "beliefs" in which something is "believed" in the way of not being completely believed.[20] Hence, although bad faith and a mere belief *simpliciter* both aim to produce beliefs without having sufficient evidence, bad faith has its own unique feature: It aims to produce quasi-beliefs, which, strictly speaking, are not mere beliefs *simpliciter*, but *mere beliefs in the degenerate form*.

The characteristic of the category of distortions in bad faith is, therefore, a quite peculiar one: In bad faith we aim to distort something in the sense that we *determine in advance* that we will not be fully convinced in order to "convince" ourselves of the distorted result. This echoes one point that I raised earlier, that in bad faith we can never completely succeed in deceiving ourselves. This inevitable result of bad faith, which might seem surprising and was perhaps hard to understand when we used the metaphor of lying in general to approximate bad faith, is no longer so. For if, in bad faith, we determine *a priori* that non-persuasion is the essential structure of the "convictions" that we are after, the result of not completely believing what we believe is exactly what we want![21]

Bad faith is faith, because it tries to produce beliefs without having enough evidence. Yet it is a special kind of faith, because not only does it end up with not believing what it believes, but also, it does not *wish* to believe fully what it tries to believe at the very beginning. It is this feature that essentially distinguishes bad faith from a knowing belief, a mere belief *simpliciter*, and good faith. But what is the condition of the possibility of having that feature? Where do we gain the justification for adopting such a peculiar move in the project of bad faith?

A glimpse at the structure of mere beliefs will provide us the answer.

When we reflect upon the structure of mere beliefs, we find that every mere belief is self-destructive in nature—it exists only insofar as it denies itself. And, it is precisely this feature, the self-destructive nature of mere beliefs, that is presupposed by bad faith and used as the justificatory ground for willingly not-believing-what-one-believes. But how should we understand the self-destructive nature of mere beliefs? And why do mere beliefs have such a characteristic?

Carole Haynes-Curtis, in her article "The 'Faith' of Bad Faith," suggested that the self-destructive nature of mere beliefs is nothing other than that if one chooses to attribute the status of mere belief to something on the reflective level, by the very act of choosing to call it mere belief rather than knowledge, and by the reflective awareness that the so-called mere belief is not grounded in evidence, he or she can at any time choose not to believe it.[22] But I think that this explanation of the self-destructive nature of mere beliefs by appealing to one's choice of certain understanding *on the reflective level* is not what Sartre had in mind when he said:

> To believe is to know that one believes, and to know that one believes is no longer to believe. . . . To be sure, . . . non-thetic consciousness is not to know. But it is in its very translucency at the origin of all knowing. Thus the non-thetic consciousness (of) believing is destructive of belief. . . . [T]he being of consciousness is to exist by itself, then to make itself be and thereby to pass beyond itself. In this sense consciousness is perpetually escaping itself, belief becomes non-belief, the immediate becomes mediation, the absolute becomes relative, and the relative becomes absolute. (EN, 110; BN, 114–15)

It is no doubt true that if I am reflectively aware that I believe something without having sufficient evidence, I can choose not to believe it, as Haynes-Curtis claimed. Nevertheless, what Sartre really meant in the above passage is something different: Whether or not I am reflectively aware of the "believing" project, my mere belief *itself* is self-destructive, that is, it can only exist as its non-positional awareness (of) itself, and this non-positional awareness (of) itself inevitably alters itself. How should we understand that?

Mere belief is a project of making believing. The goal or end of making believing is believing, that is, non-positional "feel" (of) believing. But when we reach the end, that is, we are the non-positional "feel" (of) believing, believing cannot stabilize itself. For in the project of mere belief, the non-positional "feel" that I make myself believe is present all along, and when I reach the end—i.e., I am the non-positional "feel" (of) believing—I am also the non-positional "feel" that believing is made to be, which "feel" destabilizes the end I reach—the believing. In this sense, mere belief can be understood as a self-destructive project.

This self-destructive character of mere belief provides us another way to understand the paradoxical doctrine. In those consciousnesses (including mere beliefs) that aim to make themselves to be certain non-positional "feels," consciousness is what it is not and is not what it is. Consciousness is what it is not in the sense that consciousness tries to become a certain non-positional "feel," which it is not yet. And consciousness is not what it is in the sense that in being the non-positional "feel," consciousness cannot maintain and stabilize itself because of the "feel" that consciousness is made to be.

Thus, we have worked out the second presupposition of bad faith: Bad faith presupposes and uses the fact that mere belief is self-destructive.

The Third Presupposition of Bad Faith

The third condition presupposed by bad faith, according to Sartre in *Section III* of the chapter on bad faith, is that the project of good faith can never successfully achieve its goal.

Although Sartre spent only a few passages in discussing good faith in *Being and Nothingness*, he used the term 'good faith' in at least two senses: Sometimes he took it to mean the project whose goal is the in-itself* of any mere belief (e.g., my belief that Pierre feels friendship for me), and sometimes he took it to mean the project whose goal is the in-itself* of the mere belief that asserts that I am the in-itself* that I am not in the way of being what I am not (e.g., that I am a brave man when I act courageously). Since the latter occurs in the context where Sartre contrasted good faith with bad faith, and since in those passages where Sartre discussed good faith his major aim was to shed light on the ontological structures of bad faith through the contrast and connection between good faith and bad faith, I think that we should take good faith in the second sense.

It is not hard to observe that bad faith presupposes good faith and uses a certain feature of good faith to justify a move it adopts in its project. Before bad faith affects itself with the quasi-belief that it desires, it performs a move in which it disarms all beliefs in advance, including those that it wishes to take hold of and those that it wishes to flee (EN, 110–11;

BN, 115). To justify that move, bad faith relies on understanding from two aspects: 1. As far as the structure of mere beliefs is concerned, all beliefs should have the same status, because they are all self-destructive. 2. As far as the project of good faith is concerned, all mere beliefs still have the same status. "2" might not seem to be obvious at first sight, because good faith apparently tries to get hold of *some* mere beliefs, while bypassing others. But since the project of good faith is doomed to fail due to the unachievable goal that it has, "every belief in good faith is an impossible belief" (EN, 110; BN, 115), and consequently, the mere beliefs that good faith tries to get hold of could be put on a par with the mere beliefs that it bypasses, insofar as the two groups of mere beliefs are both "impossible."[23] Thus, we see how bad faith uses the inevitable failure of good faith to justify one of the moves that it adopts, the move of disarming all mere beliefs.

Good faith is presupposed and used by bad faith in the project of bad faith. This notwithstanding, does good faith have the same structure as bad faith? Commentators such as Ronald Santoni and Joseph Catalano thought that Sartre was not always consistent on this point in *Being and Nothingness*. Whereas at various places Sartre (correctly) distinguished good faith from bad faith, Sartre's remark that good faith takes the in-itself* of believing what one believes as its goal, according to Santoni and Catalano, nonetheless makes good faith indistinguishable from bad faith.[24] To support the last claim, they reasoned as follows: Because at the end of *section III* of the chapter on bad faith, Sartre drew an analogy between good faith and "sincerity" when he said that "[t]he ideal of good faith (to believe what we believe) is, like that of sincerity (to be what one is), an ideal of being-in-itself" (EN, 110; BN, 115), and since "the essential structure of sincerity does not differ from that of bad faith" (EN, 105; BN, 109), good faith must have the same structure as bad faith.

Nevertheless, it seems to me that Santoni's and Catalano's interpretations are wrong, and Sartre was consistent all along in separating good faith from bad faith in *Being and Nothingness*. Particularly, I disagree with Santoni and Catalano about their claim that having the in-itself* as its goal would make good faith indistinguishable from bad faith. For it seems to me that their reasoning upon which this claim is based contains a problematic presupposition that the crucial factor that makes a (certain type of) "sincerity" indistinguishable from bad faith is what "sincerity" and good faith have in common—having the goal of the in-itself*. But this presupposition is obviously false, for if the character of having the in-itself* as its goal were what it takes to make a behavior bad faith, then every unreflective consciousness would have to be in bad faith, which Sartre didn't seem to hold. Indeed, when Sartre discussed "sincerity" on a par with bad faith, what makes "sincerity" indistinguishable from bad faith is the fact that in certain projects of "sincerity" the sincerity intention is used as a stepping-stone to achieve the opposite of sincerity, not the fact that bad faith and "sincerity" both have in-itself*s as their goals (EN, 102–8; BN, 106–12). The move of distorting and using the sincerity intention certainly presup-poses that the goal of "sincerity" is the in-itself*, but it goes far beyond that.

Good faith should be appropriately distinguished from bad faith, and their differences are instructive for us to understand the essential structures of bad faith. However, before we spell them out, let us first contrast good faith with a mere belief *simpliciter*. The difference between good faith and a mere belief *simpliciter* is this: A mere belief, as I said in the previous section, is a project that aims to be the non-positional "feel" (of) belief *at the non-positional side*. Good faith, however, instead of presenting the non-positional "feel" (of) belief as its goal at the non-positional side, presents the in-itself* of belief as the goal to be achieved *at the positional side*. Hence, like the project of "sincerity," the project of good faith is fundamen-tally a project of "making to be the in-itself*."[25] And because good faith presents the in-itself* of believing what it believes as its goal, we might say that good faith aims to produce mere beliefs *in the ideal form*.[26] This can be contrasted with bad faith, for the goal of bad faith is to produce quasi-beliefs, mere beliefs *in the degenerate form*.

Thus, we have encountered the first difference between good faith and bad faith: Although they are both faith (because they both try to hold beliefs without having sufficient evidence), they fundamentally differ in the nature of their respective faith. Good faith determines the nature of its faith to be believing something in the form of believing what one believes, whereas bad faith determines the nature of its faith to be believing something in the form of not quite believing what one believes. Hence, "Good faith seeks to flee the inner disintegration of my being [not-believing-what-one-believes] in the direction of the in-itself which it should be and is not [the in-itself* of belief]. Bad faith seeks to flee the in-itself by means of the inner disintegration of my being" (EN, 111; BN, 116). Moreover, good faith and bad faith also differ in the attitudes they adopt toward the determinations of their projects (i.e., the nature of faith). Good faith sincerely believes its determination of its project, whereas bad faith is *from the very start* in bad faith with respect to its determination of its project: It does not even dare to present its project to itself, let alone believing its project sincerely or insincerely. In this sense, "[t]he decision to be in bad faith does not dare to speak its name; it believes itself and does not believe itself in bad faith; it believes itself and does not believe itself in good faith" (EN, 108; BN, 113).

Good faith differs from bad faith not only in the nature of faith and in the attitude that it adopts toward its own project, but also in the *content* of the mere belief (or the quasi-belief in the case of bad faith) that it tries to produce. The mere belief that good faith tries to produce asserts that I am *the in-itself* which I am not in the way of being what I am not*[27] (e.g., the in-itself* of a coward *when I act cowardly*), whereas the quasi-belief that bad faith tries to produce asserts that I am *the in-itself* which I am not in the way of not being what I am not* (e.g., the in-itself* of a brave man *when I act cowardly*). In other words, as far as an instantaneous conscious act is concerned,[28] good faith aims to believe that I am the in-itself* that the conscious act is not in the way of being what it is not (e.g., the in-itself* identified by the exhibited behavior associated with the conscious act), whereas bad faith aims to deny that I am the in-itself* that the conscious act is not in the way of being what it is not, and to believe that I am some other in-itself* that the conscious act is not in the way of not being what it is not (i.e., the in-itself* that is not associated with the instantaneous conscious act). In sum, in contradistinction to good faith, bad faith seeks to escape from "the in-itself which I am not in the mode of being what one is not" (EN, 111; BN, 116), and aims at "the in-itself which I am not in the mode of 'not-being-what-one-is-not'" (EN, 111; BN, 116).

By means of the foregoing analysis, we are now in a position to give a complete description of the structures of bad faith. In general, the project of bad faith has two main characteristics: 1. Bad faith is fundamentally a project of quasi-belief. It determines the nature of its project as follows: Non-persuasion is the structure of the conviction that it desires, and quasi-beliefs are the beliefs it tries to affect itself with. Moreover, bad faith is from the start in bad faith with respect to its determination of the project, because it does not dare to present its project to itself. 2. Bad faith affects itself with only those beliefs that assert that I am the in-itself* that I am not in the way of not-being-what-I-am-not, while it flees those beliefs that assert that I am the in-itself* that I am not in the way of being-what-I-am-not.

"1" is possible only because every mere belief is self-destructive. "2" presupposes several things. First, it presupposes that mere beliefs are possible. We know that bad faith is faith, and it tries to produce beliefs without having sufficient evidence. But that is possible only because we can have mere beliefs, beliefs not completely fulfilled by evidence. Certainly this is not to say that the goal of bad faith is just to produce mere beliefs *simpliciter*. As we have seen, the goal of bad faith is to produce quasi-beliefs, mere beliefs in the degenerate form. However, in order for me to affect myself with quasi-beliefs, I need to imitate or simply go through the usual procedure of producing mere beliefs (but certainly I do not stop there in bad faith), since a quasi-belief is at least partly modeled after a mere belief. Hence, bad faith presupposes and uses the possibility of our having mere beliefs in a significant sense, insofar as it installs and integrates the procedure of producing mere beliefs as a constitutive component of its overall project. Moreover, in the process of producing quasi-beliefs, bad faith has to go through two stages: At the first stage, it disarms every mere belief in advance, and this presupposes and uses the fact that every mere belief is self-destructive and the fact that good faith can never achieve its goal. At the second stage, when it affects itself with the belief that I am the in-itself* that I am not in the way of not-being-what-I-am-not, bad faith presupposes and uses the fact that consciousness is not what it is and is what it is not in the project of "making to be the in-itself*."

The Ethical Implication of Bad Faith

Finally, let me discuss some implications of my interpretation, in contrast to those of Santoni's. According to Santoni, the ontological characteristics of bad faith and the contrast between good faith and bad faith have salient and non-trivial ethical implications, because bad faith is an ontological attitude of fleeing one's freedom and responsibility, whereas good faith is an attitude of accepting one's freedom and responsibility. In other words,

> While the attitude of bad faith (and sincerity) is to "miss itself" and its chosen intent, the attitude of good faith is to confront itself, not miss itself and its choices. While the attitude of bad faith is to flee its freedom and its anguish, the attitude of good faith is to face its freedom of consciousness; . . . While bad faith both exploits and pursues the impossible goal of attaining oneness with one's beliefs—of attaining coincidence with consciousness—good faith, aware of the impossibility of faith's ideal, confronts its freedom, accepts the "interrogation" or "distance" within all consciousness, refuses to *pursue* faith's impossible ideal, and accepts

responsibility for the choices it makes towards its own non-coincidence.[29]

To determine whether Santoni's interpretation is correct, we need to consider whether it fits into Sartre's theory in *Being and Nothingness*.[30]

First, Santoni's claim that in contradistinction to bad faith, good faith recognizes its freedom and takes responsibility for its acts, does not seem to be supported by textual evidence in *Being and Nothingness*. In the paradigmatic instances of good faith, for example, the mere belief that Pierre feels friendship for me (EN, 109; BN, 114), and the belief that I am not a coward when I am not cowardly in the way of not-being-what-one-is-not (EN, 107; BN, 111), Sartre did not say that the agents of good faith recognize their freedom.

Second, in the passage quoted above, Santoni seemed to take 'freedom' in the sense of non-self-identity in the being of consciousness. However, with 'freedom' understood in this sense, Santoni's claim that in contradistinction to bad faith, good faith recognizes its freedom and takes responsibility for its act is simply false. For it is bad faith, rather than good faith, that wills the disintegration of belief—the hypostatization of nothingness in its primitive project—and hence remains more intimate with freedom.

Although the contrast between good faith and bad faith should not be understood as a contrast between the ontological attitudes of accepting and fleeing one's freedom and responsibility, we cannot yet conclude that the contrast between good faith and bad faith and the ontological characteristics of bad faith do not have salient and non-trivial ethical implications, because we have not examined the ethical implications of the contrast between good faith and bad faith or the ontological characteristics of bad faith. Let us then consider them respectively.

The two differences between good faith and bad faith that we worked out before, the difference in the nature of faith and the difference in the content of belief, do not seem to carry ethical implications. For they do not seem to imply that one sort of faith distorts reality more severely than the other. Thus, the contrast between good faith and bad faith in terms of these two differences does not seem to be ethically significant. However, is there any other way, an ethically significant way, to contrast good faith with bad faith? In other words, is there any ontological characteristic that can account for the fact that bad faith is *bad* and good faith is *good*?

The only thing that I can think of is the following: In the project of bad faith, we can see two contradictory acts: On the one hand, bad faith tries to get hold of certain mere beliefs that it desires; on the other hand, by willing not-believing-what-it-believes, it ruins all mere beliefs, including those it tries to get hold of. Now, to balance itself between the two acts, bad faith creates a goal that *purports* to synthesize the opposing results of the two acts, that is, bad faith determines in advance that its goal is to affect itself with a quasi-belief, not the being of belief (non-positional "feel" [of] belief), not the in-itself* of belief, not even the nothingness of belief, but a "being" that has only an imaginary existence, and is even more grotesque than a magical being (e.g., God—a combination of the in-itself and the for-itself). Hence, in this respect, bad faith distorts reality more severely than good faith does, and accordingly, it is bad in comparison with good faith.

Although bad faith is bad and good faith good in the above sense, they both fundamentally involve "corrupted" modes of being. For (1) the goal of good faith—the in-itself* of belief—and what bad faith wills—not-believing-what-one-believes—are both *fragments* of the being of belief, and ontologically speaking cannot be separated from the totality—the being of belief, and (2) both good faith and bad faith flee what they cannot flee. With respect to "(1)," we might say the following: Good faith, by presenting the in-itself* of belief as its goal, distorts the being of belief, insofar as good faith tries to separate the in-itself* of belief from the being of belief in order to present the in-itself* of belief as its goal. Bad faith, by willing not-believing-what-one-believes (separately from the being of belief), behaves as if it tried to hypostatize the nothingness of belief, as if it tried to positivize the pure negativity of the original distance in the being of consciousness. With respect to "(2)," we might say the following: Good faith, by presenting the in-itself* of belief as its goal, keeps itself blind to the nothingness of belief—one of the defining characteristics of the being of belief. Bad faith flees what it cannot flee—the in-itself* that I am not in the way of being what I am not (e.g., the in-itself* of a coward when I act cowardly). For when I affect myself with bad faith, I am still a coward if I act cowardly. Thus, in the above sense, good faith and bad faith are both *bad*, insofar as they both involve the distorted understanding of the being of consciousness.[31]

But if this is correct, and if the ethically significant contrast between *good* faith and *bad* faith is only made and understood within the background that they are both bad in a fundamental way, it seems that only in a meager and relative sense should we prefer good faith to bad faith ethically. Hence, the contrast between good faith and bad faith does not have *salient* ethical implication.

Moreover, because bad faith and good faith both involve corrupted modes of being, in awakening to "authenticity," we give up bad faith as well as good faith and any conscious act that involves "impure reflections."[32] Hence, it is not the ontological characteristic that belongs exclusively to bad faith, but the characteristic that is shared by bad faith, good faith, and the conscious act that involves impure reflections, that is ethically negative. Hence, the ontological characteristics of bad faith, as stated in *Being and Nothingness*, have only *trivial* ethical implication.

It is no doubt true that bad faith remains as a key notion throughout Sartre's ontology and ethics in his early philosophy: In the ontological studies in *Being and Nothingness*, bad faith provides an excellent angle to reveal the inner structures of consciousness. In the ethical studies in *Notebooks*, bad faith serves as a paradigmatic case to illustrate the unauthentic way of living. Nevertheless, the link between the ontological characteristics and the ethical status of bad faith is perhaps not so tight and significant as we normally think it to be.[33]

Notes

1. E.g., see Ronald Santoni, *Bad Faith, Good Faith, and Authenticity in Sartre's Early Philosophy*, xxxi; and see also Anderson, *Sartre's Two Ethics*, chapters 1–4.

2. What is the relation between bad faith and the project of bad faith? Bad faith is a consciousness that has several distinctive features. The project of bad faith is bad faith understood in a way that emphasizes the non-positional "feel" (of) bad faith as a complex involving goals, plans, and deliberating efforts.

3. For example, see Jeffrey Gordon, "Bad Faith: A Dilemma," *Philosophy* 60 (1985): 258–62.

4. In the text of *Being and Nothingness*, Sartre used 'falsehood' or 'ideal lie' interchangeably for 'lying in general'.

5. Briefly, Sartre's reason for distinguishing lying to oneself from lying in general is as follows: Lying in general requires a deceiver and a deceived, and has the structure that the deceiver knows the truth and the deceived does not know the truth. However, in the project of lying to oneself, because the deceiver and the deceived are one, and a person cannot both *know* and *not know* the truth at the same time, the project could not have the structure of lying in general. It might be thought that in the project of lying to oneself, since a person is always non-positionally aware (of) the truth, he or she might be said to know and not to know the truth at the same time. However, this inference is clearly invalid. If we take 'knowing' to mean

knowledge*, then the person cannot be said to know the truth, since non-positional awareness is not knowledge*. And if we take 'knowing' to mean non-positional awareness, then the person cannot be said not to know the truth. Hence, in lying to oneself, we do not have an impossible situation where a person both knows and does not know the truth at the same time *in the same sense of "knowing."*.

6.   After distinguishing lying to oneself from a strict lie, I shall follow Sartre in treating 'bad faith' and 'lying to oneself' as interchangeable terms. (Again, here the term 'lying to oneself' is just a piece of Sartrean terminology, which does not carry the sense of an ordinary lie.) Once we do that, "(1)" is just the claim that bad faith is ontologically impossible.

7.   To my knowledge, Leslie Stevenson is the first one who argued at some length that the waiter does not *have to be* in bad faith in the example (see Leslie Stevenson, "Sartre on Bad Faith," *Philosophy* 58 [1983]: 256). Although I agree with Stevenson on this point, in this chapter I want to argue for something different, that the waiter example was not *intended* by Sartre as an illustration of the patterns of bad faith, whether or not the waiter really is or has to be in bad faith in the example.

8.   It seems to me that the waiter does not *have to be* in bad faith in the example. But it is beyond the scope of this chapter to argue for that in detail.

9.   In *Being and Nothingness* 'in-itself' is certainly the technical term that refers to the stuff that limits our freedom. However, at many places Sartre used the word 'in-itself' in the sense of things, including physical things, imaginary entities, social positions, etc. In this book I call "in-itself" in the sense of things "in-itself*." Although in-itself* is not exactly in-itself, in-itself* share with in-itself the properties of "in-itself[*] is," "in-itself[*] is in-itself," "in-itself[*] is what it is."

10.   The project of "making to be the in-itself*" can be taken in two senses: In the narrow sense, it denotes those projects in which the in-itself* is presented as a goal, as a transcendent being of positional consciousness (e.g., the project of becoming sadness). In the broad sense, it denotes not only what it denotes in the narrow sense, but also any conscious act that has certain exhibited behavior associated with it (e.g., the conscious act associated with cowardly behavior). Clearly we need this broad sense of 'making to be the in-itself*' in *Being and Nothingness*, because in the coward example, an example of "making to be the in-itself*," the person who acts cowardly does not *have to* present the in-itself* of a coward as his or her goal, as an object of positional consciousness. My focus in the paper is the broad sense of "making to be the in-itself*."

11.   For example, "[i]f I make myself sad, I must continue to make myself sad from beginning to end. I can not treat my sadness as an impulse finally achieved and put it on file without recreating it, nor can I carry it in the manner of an inert body which continues its movement after the initial shock" (EN, 101; BN, 104).

12.   For example, to make myself to be the conscious state "sadness," I have to affect myself with sadness, and yet by the non-positional awareness (of) the affecting act, I "know" that I am not sad, and hence, "the being of sadness escapes

me by and in the very act by which I affect myself with it" (EN, 101; BN, 104).

13. The "is" (or "is not") in the slogan should be distinguished from "is" in a statement about things (in-itself*s). When Sartre said that consciousness *is* what it is not, the copula "is" should not be understood as referring to a way of "being in-itself*," but as referring to a way of qualifiedly realizing the in-itself*. (Similarly, when Sartre said that consciousness *is not* what it is, "is not" should not be understood as referring to a way of "a thing's not being another thing.")

14. E.g., the distorted understanding of the transcendence/facticity distinction and the being-for-itself/being-for-others distinction, the declaration of not being the homosexual in the sense of "not-being-in-itself," and the denial of being a coward.

15. The "sincerity" that Sartre discussed in the text certainly is not the honest behavior that innocently confesses one's past deeds and intentions (EN, 106; BN, 110). What he had in mind is rather the behavior that uses the sincerity intention to achieve the opposite of sincerity, which *does not* coincide with what we ordinarily understand as sincerity in the innocent sense.

16. In the homosexual example, although the critic of the homosexual does not try to escape from his own being, he does strive to make his opponent escape from the homosexual deeds.

17. I think that these questions are roughly what Sartre had in mind when he said: "We have indicated for the moment only those conditions which render bad faith conceivable, the structures of being which permit us to form concepts of bad faith. We can not limit ourselves to these considerations; we have not yet distinguished bad faith from falsehood" (EN, 108; BN, 112).

18. Careless readers of Sartre might quickly equate bad faith with a mere belief *simpliciter* when they read Sartre's remark that ". . .bad faith is belief; and the essential problem of bad faith is a problem of belief" (EN, 108; BN, 112). However, when Sartre went on to analyze the structures of the project of bad faith, he clearly distinguished bad faith from a mere belief *simpliciter.*

19. This is obvious, because in bad faith we do need some kind of justification (e.g., the understanding of the contradictory nature of consciousness) rather than no justification at all to form false beliefs.

20. In other words, "[b]ad faith apprehends evidence but it is resigned in advance to not being fulfilled by this evidence, to not being persuaded and transformed into good faith. . . . It stands forth in the firm resolution *not to demand too much*, to count itself satisfied when it is barely persuaded, to force itself in decisions to adhere to uncertain truth" (EN, 109; BN, 113).

21. Similar things can be said about the evanescent feature of bad faith. Bad faith can determine its structure to be metastable, so it will not be surprised at the fact that it is evanescent. Sartre did not explicitly say this, but it was almost there.

22. Particularly, Haynes-Curtis said: "Sartre further complicates the matter by coupling with the thought that beliefs are chosen, the idea that to acknowledge belief is in some way to negate it. Sartre says, 'To believe is to know that one believes, and to know that one believes is no longer to believe'. What I take Sartre

to mean here is that once, on the reflective level, I choose to give the status of belief to my feelings on the pre-reflective level, by the very act of choosing to call this belief and not knowledge, then I can at any time choose not to believe it" (Carole Haynes-Curtis, "The 'Faith' of Bad Faith," *Philosophy* 63 [1988]: 270). However, it seems to me that Haynes-Curtis' extrapolation cannot be right, since immediately after saying that "[t]o believe is to know that one believes, and to know that one believes is no longer to believe," Sartre hastened to add that this is only a forced description of the phenomenon designated with the term 'to know', and that what he really intended by "knowing" is but the non-thetic consciousness (EN, 110; BN, 114).

23. Certainly, the two groups of mere beliefs are *impossible* in different senses. For the mere beliefs that good faith tries to get hold of are impossible because of the inevitable failure of the project of good faith, whereas the mere beliefs that good faith bypasses are impossible simply because good faith does not try to get hold of them. However, since bad faith demands only non-persuasive evidence, the conflation of the two senses of "impossibility" is excusable for bad faith.

24. See Santoni, *Bad Faith*, 73–74. See also Joseph Catalano, "On the Possibility of Good Faith," *Man and World* 13 (1980): 211.

25. It is so, according to my definition of the project of "making to be the in-itself*" in note 10.

26. The goal of good faith, the in-itself* of believing what one believes, can be understood as the ideal form of a mere belief because it is the "belief-God" that stabilizes itself.

27. This expression is equivalent to the expression that the belief that good faith tries to produce asserts that I am *the in-itself* which I am in the way of not being what I am*, because we know that in the project of "making to be the in-itself*," consciousness is the in-itself* in the way of not being what it is, and is not the in-itself* in the way of being what it is not.

28. Here what I mean by "conscious act" is an act that has certain exhibited behavior associated with it. Hence, it can be viewed as a project of "making to be the in-itself*."

29. Santoni, *Bad Faith*, 80–81.

30. It is obvious that Santoni cannot *wholly* rely on Sartre's *Notebooks for an Ethics* to vindicate his interpretation, for various reasons. One apparent reason is that in *Notebooks for an Ethics* at various places Sartre seemed to treat 'good faith' as synonymous with 'authenticity' (NE, 12), which contradicts one of Santoni's other major theses, that good faith is significantly different from authenticity (Santoni, *Bad Faith*, chapter 6).

31. I suggest that it is in this sense that we should understand the well-known, baffling footnote on "authenticity" and the contrast between two immediate attitudes (not as a contrast between a correct and an incorrect attitudes, but as a contrast between two paradigmatic forms of distortion).

32. This is also true in the transition from "natural freedom" to "ethical

freedom" in de Beauvoir's "ethics of ambiguity." See Simone de Beauvoir, *The Ethics of Ambiguity* (New York: Citadel Press, 1962), 24–26.

33. A similar thing might be said about good faith, but it is more likely that Sartre significantly changed his notion of "good faith" when his interest shifted from the ontological inquiries in *Being and Nothingness* to the ethical investigations in *Notebooks for an Ethics*.

Chapter Five

Pure Reflection in Sartre's
Being and Nothingness

Introduction

The purpose of this chapter is twofold. Through an interpretation of Sartre's theory of "pure reflection" that he presented in *Being and Nothingness*, I want to show that (1) Sartre's theory of pure reflection is more subtle than most commentators take it to be, and (2) a philosophical method including pure reflection as a component satisfies a basic requirement for any *sound* philosophical method, the requirement that the philosophical method produces universal knowledge, the universality of which is not empirical universality.

"Pure reflection" is an important concept that bridges Sartre's ontology and ethics in his early philosophy. In *Being and Nothingness*, Sartre spent a section (*part two, chapter two, section III*) discussing the ontological characteristics of pure reflection. In *Notebooks for an Ethics*, Sartre explored the ethical implications of the ontological characteristics of pure reflection (that he presented in *Being and Nothingness*), and he used pure reflection as an essential stage leading to an ethical life of "authenticity."

"Pure reflection" is also *the* central notion in Sartre's philosophical methodology. When Sartre presented his theory of pure reflection in *Being and Nothingness* (and an analog of it in *The Transcendence of the Ego*[1]), his concern was purely methodological—through a presentation of the ontological characteristics of pure reflection, Sartre tried to work out a reliable method that enabled him to make, justifiably, all of the claims about consciousness that he made in *Being and Nothingness*.[2,3]

Many commentators have recognized the importance of pure reflection in Sartre's ethics. But few have appreciated the importance of pure reflection in Sartre's philosophical methodology.[4] Partly due to this negligence, Sartre's discussion of the ontological characteristics of pure reflection in *Being and Nothingness* have not been studied closely. But without a thorough understanding of the ontological characteristics of pure reflection, not only do we fail to appreciate Sartre's philosophical method, but also, we lack the ground to understand the ethical implications of pure reflection and subsequently Sartre's early ethics as a whole. To appreciate Sartre's philosophical method and to obtain the ground to understand the ethical implications of pure reflection, I pursue a detailed study of the ontological characteristics of pure reflection that Sartre presented in *Being and Nothingness*.

But my purpose is not merely exegetic. Through a clarification of Sartre's theory of pure reflection, I argue that pure reflection yields *normative universal knowledge* in contrast to *scientific, empirical knowledge*. On the basis of that, I argue that if a philosophical method includes pure reflection as a component, it satisfies a necessary condition for soundness, that the philosophical method produces universal knowledge, the universality of which is not empirical universality.

Husserl's Phenomenological *Epoché*

I shall start with Husserl's phenomenological *epoché*, because (1) Husserl's phenomenological method[5] deeply influenced Sartre, (2) phenomenological *epoché* and pure reflection play roughly[6] the same role in Husserl's and Sartre's philosophies, and (3) some recent commentaries on pure reflection (e.g., Thomas Busch's) equate pure reflection with the phenomenological *epoché*.[7] In the following, I will discuss the procedure and the motivation of the phenomenological *epoché* respectively.[8]

First, the procedure. On the negative side, the phenomenological *epoché* presents a systematic way to bracket everything that is "transcendent." On the positive side, the phenomenological *epoché* opens up a field of "immanence" for study. Husserl used the word 'immanent' (and 'transcendent'[9]) in three senses: (1) an intentional object is immanent if and only if it is fully evidentially grasped in the consciousness that is conscious of the object;[10] (2) an intentional object is immanent if and only if it is literally contained in the consciousness that is conscious of the object;[11] (3) an intentional object is immanent if and only if it belongs to the same conscious stream that includes the consciousness that is conscious of the object.[12,13] Husserl touched briefly on (1) and (2) in *The Idea of Phenomen-*

ology, but he rejected both in his later works.[14] He rejected (1) because it mistakenly includes essences in the realm of immanence; he rejected (2) because it captures only the sense of immanent object in what Husserl later called "perception of something immanent,"[15] but not the sense of immanent object in general. Hereafter let me follow the later Husserl to use 'immanent' (and 'transcendent') in the last sense only.

Husserl called the field of immanence (which the phenomenological *epoché* opens up) a realm of *cogitationes*. The *cogitationes* are *not* our actual unreflected[16] mental processes, but "parallelized" and reconstructed counterparts of the actual unreflected mental processes.[17] Whereas an actual unreflected mental process is a "Heraclitean flux,"[18] a "flow of retentions and protentions,"[19] which exhibits no correlative poles such as *noesis* (roughly, the constituting acts) and *noema* (the constituted objects),[20] the *cogitationes* are our reconstructions of the actual unreflected mental processes; and these reconstructions exhibit the *noema/noesis* structure. Moreover, Husserl took *noesis* as the really inherent moment of a *cogitatio*; that moment includes the hyletic material and the synthesizing principle[21] and is united by the transcendental ego. Thus, a *cogitatio* is a complex, consisting of three elements: the hyletic material, the synthesizing principle, and the transcendental ego. Without going into further details about the *noesis* and *noema*, let me stress here that Husserl made a distinction ·between our actual unreflected mental processes and their reconstructions in Husserlian reflection, and he used the phenomenological *epoché* to steer us to the field of the *reconstructed* mental processes, rather than the realm of the actual *unreflected* mental processes.

Next, the motivation. Why did Husserl perform the phenomenological *epoché*? Husserl's answer is that consciousness of something transcendent is epistemologically "flawed" in the sense of lacking "apodictic evidence," whereas consciousness of something immanent is not. And Husserl wanted "apodictic evidence" because he wanted philosophy to be a rigorous science and rigorous sciences are "apodictic." For Husserl, a consciousness has apodictic evidence only if it is immune to errors from illusion[22] and adumbration.[23] I shall discuss these errors in the following.

A common case of illusion is sensory illusion. We know that our senses can "deceive" us, and the causes of errors come either from the world (e.g., our seeing a bent oar in the water) or from ourselves (e.g., our having hallucinations due to taking drugs). There are, however, other sorts of illusion as well; for example, I thought that I solved a difficult logical problem yesterday but I just found out that a wrong inference was made in the proof. In general, an error from illusion can take place whenever (1) we have a consciousness *with a transcendent, intentional object* and (2) in that consciousness our positing of the existence and/or properties of the object is *corrigible*. Given this understanding of illusion, the only consciousness that is immune to errors from illusion—if it exists[24]—is the immediate introspection whose intentional object is a fragment of a *cogitatio*, i.e., *this* momentary experience *here and now*.[25]

To understand errors from adumbration, we need to understand Husserl's adumbration thesis that a perceptual, transcendent object is always given to us in profiles. This thesis can have a weak and a strong version. In the weak version,[26] it means that when we are conscious of a perceptual, transcendent object, there is no single conscious act in which we can posit the existence of the object with certainty. (E.g., with respect to any of my perceptual consciousnesses of a cube, there are always sides of the cube that I don't see.[27]) Note that this does not imply that we *cannot* know for certain the existence of a perceptual, transcendent object in any case, because although no single consciousness enables us to posit the existence of a certain object with certainty, a finite set of consciousnesses might suffice. (E.g., when I have seen and touched every side of a cube, I might posit the existence of the cube with certainty.[28,29]) In the strong version, the one Sartre attributed to Husserl (EN, 12–14; BN, 5–7) and the one Husserl held at one point, the thesis means that in any consciousness (or any finite set of consciousnesses) wherein we posit the existence of a certain perceptual object, our positing act is not fully evidentially grounded. For in that consciousness (or the finite set of consciousnesses), we have infinite anticipations of the appearances of the object that are unfulfilled.[30] Moreover, we have infinite unfulfilled anticipations because the very meaning of the posited object is "an infinite idea related to infinities of harmoniously combinable experiences,"[31,32] including infinite anticipated appearances of the object. For example, when I posit a cube in a perceptual consciousness, I have infinite unfulfilled anticipations of the cube's appearances from all perspectives that I have never had before. And I have infinite anticipations of the cube's appearances, because the meaning of the cube refers to a series of infinite anticipated appearances. Obviously, in the strong version we equate *the posited perceptual object* with *the meaning of the object*, and *the meaning of the object* with *a series of the appearances of the object*.[33] In sum, in both versions there is room for error in every perceptual consciousness, because our posit of the perceptual object has to be tested by past or/and future perceptual consciousness(es).[34]

Pure Reflection in Sartre's *Being and Nothingness*

At first sight, Sartre's pure reflection is similar to Husserl's phenomenological *epoché* in its procedure and motivation. Like the phenomenological *epoché*, pure reflection has its focus on consciousness (the "for-itself"), and it marks a correct way to access our conscious life. Like the phenomenological *epoché*, pure reflection aims to generate cognition that has apodictic evidence. Nonetheless, when we look at the details, they are quite different. First, their procedures are different. Whereas the phenomenological *epoché* and pure reflection both lead to a way of introspection, the former uncovers *a reconstructed consciousness in a particular sort of reflection* (i.e., the hyletic material + the synthesizing principle + the transcendental ego), whereas the latter uncovers *an actual unreflected consciousness* (through purely reflecting on the non-positional consciousness). Second, their motivations are different. Whereas both the phenomenological *epoché* and pure reflection aim to generate cognition that has apodictic evidence, Sartre and Husserl wanted apodictic evidence for different reasons. For Husserl, the reason is that he wanted philosophy to be a rigorous science, and rigorous sciences are apodictic. For Sartre, the reason is that he wanted to uncover the being of consciousness (the unreflected consciousness), and it is only through reflection with apodictic evidence (pure reflection) that he can achieve it (EN, 197; BN, 212). As a result, in *Being and Nothingness* Sartre used the term 'apodictic evidence' in a sense different from Husserl's, a sense that has nothing to do with errors from illusion and adumbration.[35]

This said, let's explicate "pure reflection." I shall start by introducing some terminologies I will use. By "reflective" I mean the consciousness (or the part of consciousness) that is doing the job of reflecting (whether purely or not) in reflection.[36] By "reflected-on" I mean the consciousness (or the part of consciousness) that is uncovered in reflection.[37]

Now let's consider a group of what we ordinarily call "reflection" or "introspection," the group of memory-based "reflections." In those "reflections," we live *only the reflective*. When I reflect upon the toothache I had yesterday, for example, I live only the reflective, my reflecting the toothache. The reflected-on, my experience of the toothache, is something I lived yesterday but no longer live at the moment of reflection.

In pure reflection, however, things are different. We live, in pure reflection, not only the reflective *but also all moments of the reflected-on*. Consider an example of pure reflection that Sartre discussed in both *The Transcendence of Ego* and *Being and Nothingness*: I watch myself writing.[38] Here the reflective is my watching, and the reflected-on is the act of my writing. In this reflective project, I must live all moments of the act of my writing, for I cannot watch myself *writing* without my being bent over a table, moving my hand, etc. Consider another example of pure reflection. Suppose I reflect on the process of my constructing a logical proof in order to check whether the proof is correct.[39] In this case, the checking cannot be exercised without my constructing the proof step by step.

In pure reflection, although we live all moments of the reflected-on, we do not live the reflected-on (as we do outside of the context of pure reflection); rather, we live a *modification* of the reflected-on, the "reflected-on-for-a-witness" (the reflected-on modified to exist for a witness). In watching myself writing or checking a proof, I do not simply fall into an unreflected consciousness wherein I am completely absorbed in writing or constructing a proof. Instead, I am writing or constructing a proof *for a witness*. In the following let me call this modification of the reflected-on "reflected-on*."[40]

Note here the subtle relation between the reflected-on* and the reflected-on. Although the reflected-on* is not exactly the reflected-on, they are for the most part the same, except that the non-positional "feel" (of) the reflected-on* contains the extra part of "existing for a witness." In other words, the non-positional "feel" (of) the reflected-on* contains (1) everything in the non-positional "feel" (of) the reflected-on and (2) the "feel" (of) "existing for a witness." In watching myself writing, my writing for a witness (the reflected-on*) is not exactly the same as my writing in the unreflected state (the reflected-on). However, they differ only in the aspect that my writing for a witness contains the "feel" (of) "existing for a witness" that my writing in the unreflected state lacks. Insofar as the non-positional "feel" (of) the reflected-on* contains everything in the non-positional "feel" (of) the reflected-on, we say that in pure reflection, we live all moments of the reflected-on.

In connection with the distinction between the reflected-on* and the reflected-on, an important methodological question can be raised with respect to the legitimacy of Sartre's ontological remarks about the unreflected for-itself (the reflected-on): How can we know anything about the unreflected for-itself (the reflected-on), if in *Being and Nothingness* all descriptions of the unreflected for-itself are made in pure reflection, and yet in pure reflection we live and subsequently uncover the *modified* unreflected for-itself (the reflected-on*) rather than the *original* unreflected for-itself (the reflected-on)? My answer is that this question is misformulated, because it does not distinguish what we *live* in pure reflection from what we *uncover* in pure reflection. Here my point is that although we live the reflected-on* in pure reflection, *what we uncover "is" the reflected-on*, with the "is" understood *in these two senses*: (1) what we uncover is grasped *phenomenologically* as the reflected-on; and (2) what we uncover *in fact* amounts to the reflected-on. With respect to (1), *phenomenologically*, we always take what we uncover in a pure reflection (e.g., watching myself writing) as the reflected-on (e.g., my writing in the unreflected state) rather than the reflected-on* (e.g., my writing for a witness). This partly explains the fact that in everyday life we have no difficulty at all talking about the unreflected consciousness. With respect to (2), what we uncover in pure reflection *is not in fact* the entire reflected-on*; *it is rather the reflected-on* minus the non-positional "feel" (of) "existing for a witness," which amounts to the non-positional "feel" (of) reflected-on.* In sum, in any pure reflection X there is a discrepancy between the reflected-on* in X and what we uncover in X: Although we live the reflected-on* in X, what we uncover in X is grasped phenomenologically as and in fact amounts to the reflected-on. (And the reflected-on* [in X] "is" uncovered [grasped phenomenologically and equivalent to what we uncover] *only* in a different pure reflection in which we reflect on X.)[41]

Having made the above observations, let's spell out the most important feature of pure reflection. One way to put it is this: In pure reflection, we live both the reflective and the reflected-on* *in such a way that although the reflective and the reflected-on* are two distinct processes, they form a peculiar sort of unity* (EN, 197–99; BN, 212–14). This unity of the reflective and the reflected-on* lies in *their non-positional "feels."*[42] Although the "feel" (of) the reflective and the "feel" (of) the reflected-on* are different, they have essential connections: The reflected-on* does not have a self-sufficient being—it exists *for a witness* and calls upon the reflective to complete itself. In other words, with respect to its "feel," the reflected-on* exists as a lack and consequently tries to be something else—the reflective.[43] On the other hand, the "feel" (of) the reflective is that the reflective is essentially an unsaturated function, a non-self-sufficient being that can become and maintain itself as witness only through our living the reflected-on*.[44] In watching myself writing, I am both watching and writing. Yet while writing, I know that I am being watched, and indeed I am writing *in order to be watched by myself.* On the other hand, I cannot watch myself writing without moving my hand; the watching can be initiated and maintained only insofar as I start and continue to write *for a witness.* In checking a logical proof, my reflective witnessing of my constructing the proof (the reflective) and my constructing the proof for a witness (the reflected-on*) are essentially related to each other in their very being. My constructing the proof refers to the reflective witnessing, because it exists in the way of *being for a witness.* My reflective witnessing, on the other hand, can be exercised only through my constructing the proof for a witness.

To acquire a thorough understanding of the peculiar unity of the reflective and the reflected-on* and the ontological structure of pure reflection, let's observe the following:

1. In pure reflection the "feel" (of) the reflective and the "feel" (of) the reflected-on* are complementary to each other in the way that each constitutes a distinct process. This means three things:

First, in pure reflection, the reflected-on* and the reflective do not exist independently, as if we first lived the reflected-on*, and after its completion we drew a reflective eye toward it. In checking a logical proof, I do not first construct the logical proof, and then recall the process of constructing the proof. Rather, I keep drawing a reflective eye all along while I am constructing the proof. The reflective goes along with the reflected-on* in pure reflection.

Second, in pure reflection, we do not live the reflective and the reflected-on* at the same instant. The situation here is different from the dyad "reflection-reflecting"[45] in an ordinary unreflected consciousness. In the dyad we have non-positional "feel" (reflecting) and acquaintance (reflection) simultaneously, because "feel" and acquaintance are two sides of a single consciousness. However, in pure reflection, the reflective and the reflected-on* are not two sides of a single consciousness in the same way that "feel" and acquaintance are (although of course the reflective and the reflected-on* are united). They cannot pop up in my head simultaneously, insofar as we cannot busy ourselves with two *different* subject matters[46] at the same instant.

Third, *in pure reflection the reflective and the reflected-on* unfold themselves alternately in an unbroken stream.* We live the reflected-on* in the sense of living for a witness, so we shift to the reflective; but the reflective exists as an unsaturated function that calls upon the reflected-on* to complete itself—"it is-in-order-to-be the reflected-on" (EN, 202; BN, 218), which refers us to our continual living of the reflected-on*; then the reflected-on* refers us again to the reflective; and the reflective to the reflected-on*; and so on, until we have finished living the complete process of the reflected-on*. In checking a logical proof, a reflective eye needs to be kept along with my constructing the proof from beginning to end. I start by living the reflected-on*—constructing the first step(s) of inference from the premises for a witness—in order to initiate the reflective check. Then I live the reflective checking, which refers me back to the continual living of the reflected-on*—constructing a further step (further steps) for a witness—in order to maintain itself as an ongoing reflective check. Then I continue to live the reflected-on*, which refers me back to the continual living of the reflective checking. . . . Such an alternating pattern repeats itself until we have reached the last step of the proof. The length of the unit of the alternating pattern is a psychological question—it may vary from person to person, from case to case. However, the important thing to observe is that in pure reflection the reflective and the reflected-on* are united in the way that each constitutes itself as a *distinct* but not *independent* process: They are not independent of each other, because, as we have shown, each of them in its "feels" refers to the (continual) living of the other. Yet they constitute distinct processes. The reflective, at a particular moment, constitutes itself as a reflective that is both a continuation of its past (past reflective) and an anticipation of its future (future reflective), and in terms of its relation with the past and future, in its very being, the reflective distinguishes itself from the reflected-on*.[47] And the same thing can be said about the reflected-on* (EN, 203; BN, 220). In this sense, Sartre said that "it is by means of the future and the past that the reflective and the reflected-on are distinguished within the unity of their being" (EN, 203; BN, 220).[48]

2. Pure reflection is not knowledge*, insofar as (1) in pure reflection the reflective does not take a point of view on the reflected-on and (2) pure reflection has the character of what we ordinarily call "recognition" (EN, 201–2; BN, 218–19).

Knowledge*, according to Sartre, is a proper subclass[49] of acquaintances in which (subclass) we take a point of view on certain intentional objects. Here 'taking a point of view'[50] means three things: (a) the object known* is independent of the knowing* act; (b) in the knowing* act we create an "external" relation ("external" in the sense that the relation does not affect the being of the object) with the object; this relation determines my point of view; (c) taking *a* point of view suggests not only that there are other points of view but also that *other points of view are excluded.* To illustrate these, let's consider a case in which I obtain knowledge* of a pebble lying in front of me.[51] In that case, what I do is to create a relation with the pebble so that I can describe it; for example, touching it from different angles, observing it with the backlit light, etc. Here note three things: First, the pebble is independent of my action. Second, I establish a relation with the pebble, which determines the way the pebble is presented to me and which relation does not affect the being of the pebble. Third, by choosing one relation I inevitably exclude other possible relations.

Nevertheless, in pure reflection neither (b) nor (c) holds. First, (b) does not hold. For the reflected-on is not disclosed through our establishing an external relation with the reflected-on. The only relation that exists in pure reflection and that is analogous to the external relation in knowledge* is the *internal* relation between the reflective and the reflected-on*; this relation is included in the very being of the reflective and the reflected-on*. Second, (c) does not hold. The reflected-on is uncovered only through our reflective witnessing of the reflected-on*, and the relation between the reflective and the reflected-on* *does not* exclude any other possible relation. The latter is the case, simply because the relation between the reflective and the reflected-on* is internal to their beings, and *there can be no such thing as another possible relation between them.*

Because neither (b) nor (c) holds in pure reflection, the reflective does not take a point of view on the reflected-on in pure reflection.[52, 53] To capture the fact that the reflective discloses and yet does not take a point of view on the reflected-on, Sartre called the reflected-on a "quasi-object" for the reflective: the reflected-on is like an object, because it functions as *something to be uncovered* by the reflective; yet it is only a *"quasi*-object," because the reflective *does not take a point of view* on the reflected-on.

Pure reflection differs from knowledge* not only in the aspect that, in pure reflection, the reflective does not take a point of view on the reflected-on, but also in the aspect that pure reflection has the character of what we ordinarily call "recognition." Whereas in knowledge* we acquire some-thing new, in pure reflection we uncover what we are already familiar with in some way (i.e., we uncover the reflected-on that *we are non-positionally aware [of] before the reflection*), which is similar to what we do in a recognition in everyday life. In this sense, Sartre says that "[pure] reflection is a recognition" (EN, 202; BN, 219).

Furthermore, pure reflection differs from all three sorts of consciousness that Sartre discussed in *The Psychology of Imagination*: perception, imagination, and conception (PI, 3–21). Unlike perception,[54] purely reflective recognition is not liable to perceptual error, because in pure reflection, we do not *posit* the existence of the reflected-on (rather, we live all moments of the reflected-on). Unlike imagination (of physical objects),[55] it does not reveal the reflected-on in profiles, because the reflected-on is not manifested through appearances. Unlike conception,[56] it is not incomplete, because the reflective in pure reflection does not take a "perspective" on the reflected-on, as we do in conception.[57]

3. Pure reflection should be appropriately distinguished from what Sartre calls "impure reflection," a bad sort of reflection often encountered in both ordinary and philosophical thinking. Impure reflection, according to Sartre, is pure reflection plus more—and it is the "more" that makes it *impure* (EN, 201; BN, 218) (I will come back to discuss this). Impure reflection can be suitably called "self-knowledge*," since (a) it is a subclass of knowledge* and (b) in it the "I" or "Me,"[58] and/or the agent's psychic state(s), quality(ies), action(s), and the like, are posited.[59] Having discussed the differences between pure reflection and knowledge* in general, now let me contrast pure reflection with impure reflection and discuss them in regard to those features that belong to impure reflection but not necessarily to knowledge* in general.

First, we must be clear about the scope of impure and pure reflection. A consciousness is impure reflection if and only if[60] in it one or more of the transcendent "I" or "Me," the agent's state(s) (e.g., anger), the agent's quality(ies) (e.g., irascibility), the agent's act(s)[61] (e.g., doubting), or any other reconstruction of the reflected-on* that uses the model of the in-itself is posited (EN, 209; BN, 226; TL, 44–74; TE, 60–93).[62] And a consciousness is pure reflection only if it contains none of the aforementioned posits we find in impure reflection.[63]

Second, impure reflection starts with but goes beyond pure reflection. Impure reflection has to start with the reflected-on*, for without the reflected-on* it has nothing to grasp. Yet impure reflection goes beyond pure reflection, insofar as it pre-outlines an in-itself* behind the reflected-on* (EN, 207; BN, 224), "traverses the [reflected-on*] in order to recover it and to found it" (EN, 207; BN, 224–25), and gets out of the lightning intuition in pure reflection and adopts a point of view on the in-itself* behind the reflected-on* (EN, 207; BN, 225). The in-itself* that the impure reflection posits behind the reflected-on* is an "in-itself-shadow" of the reflected-on*, because it is a projection of the reflected-on* and yet it is constructed out of the properties that belong to the in-itself* (including those properties that belong to the in-itself) (EN, 207; BN, 224–25). In this sense the shadow is a "magical"[64] combination of the for-itself and the in-itself, and accordingly impure reflection is in bad faith (EN, 208; BN, 225–26). In short, impure reflection is a "projection into the in-itself on the part of the for-itself [reflected-on*]—as a meaning" (EN, 207; BN, 225).

Third, in pure reflection there is apodictic evidence, whereas in impure reflection there isn't. Sartre espoused two senses of "apodictic evidence": one in *The Transcendence of the Ego*,[65] and the other in *Being and Nothingness* (EN, 211–12; BN, 229–30). The first sense is more or less a Husserlian one: A cognitive consciousness has apodictic evidence if and only if it is immune to errors from adumbration.[66] According to this sense, in most[67] impure reflection, we do not have apodictic evidence, because in those consciousnesses we posit a perceptual object—the "Psyche"—which is uncovered in profiles.[68] In pure reflection, however, we do have apodictic evidence, because the quasi-object of the recognition—the reflected-on—is not uncovered in profiles. The second (non-Husserlian) sense has nothing to do with errors from illusion and adumbration. It is this: A reflective consciousness is apodictic if and only if in the reflection we are "certain" about the existence of the reflected-on—"certain" in the *peculiar* sense that we *live* all moments of the reflected-on in the reflection.[69] According to this sense, in impure reflection, we don't have apodictic evidence, because in impure reflection we do not and cannot live all moments of the reflected-on—the *in-itself-shadow* of the reflected-on*. In contradistinction, in pure reflection, we do have apodictic evidence, because we live all moments of the reflected-on.

4. Pure reflection has intimate relations with non-positional "feels." First of all, as I said before, it is through the non-positional "feels" (of) the reflective and the reflected-on* that the reflective and the reflected-on* are united in pure reflection. Second, pure reflection presents an analog of non-positional "feels." Like non-positional "feels," reflection (both pure and impure)[70] is an effort of consciousness to found itself.[71] Whereas a non-positional "feel" is an effort of consciousness to found itself by presenting itself to itself through the "original scissiparity" (the non-coincidence of consciousness with itself) in the being of consciousness (EN, 115–21; BN, 119–26), reflection is an effort of consciousness to found itself by making of it a given that is both *what appears to consciousness* and *what consciousness is* (EN, 200; BN, 216). To make of it a given that is an

appearance for consciousness, is to recognize the reflected-on as a quasi-object. To make of it a given that is what consciousness is, is to live or try to live all moments of the reflected-on, i.e., to reach the being of the reflected-on from inside (interiorize the given) (EN, 200; BN, 216). Third, the reflective scissiparity in pure reflection might be viewed to exist potentially in the being of the reflected-on (non-positional "feel" [of] of the reflected-on). As Sartre put it,

> This phenomenon of reflection is a permanent possibility of the for-itself because reflective scissiparity exists potentially in the for-itself which is reflected-on; it suffices in fact that the reflecting for-itself (*reflétant*) [the non-positional consciousness (of) the reflected-on] posit itself for it as a witness *of* the reflection (*reflet*) [the reflected-on] and that the for-itself (the reflection) [the reflected-on as witnessed] posit itself *for it* as a reflection of this reflecting. (EN, 201; BN, 217)

According to the passage, the reflective scissiparity in pure reflection might be viewed to exist *potentially* in the reflected-on, because although the reflective scissiparity does not actually exist in the reflected-on, it would if the reflected-on were to undergo some changes. As the second sentence (the one starting with "it suffices") says, the non-positional consciousness (of) the reflected-on would turn itself into the reflective in pure reflection if it were to change itself to be a witness of (instead of a "feel" [of]) the positional consciousness. As the third sentence (the one starting with "and that the for-itself") says, the reflected-on (as witness by the modified non-positional consciousness) would turn itself into the reflected-on* in pure reflection if it were to make itself exist for a witness. In sum, from the above we see that without non-positional "feels," without the structure of consciousness as presenting itself to itself, pure reflection cannot take place in the first place.

Empirical Universality versus Normative Universality

Having clarified Sartre's theory of pure reflection and contrasted it with Husserl's phenomenological *epoché*, I argue in this section that if a philosophical method includes pure reflection as a component, it satisfies a basic requirement for any sound philosophical method, namely, the requirement that the philosophical method produces universal knowledge, the universality of which is not empirical universality.[72]

I start with a simple truism that philosophy, like most empirical sciences, produces universal knowledge—knowledge that says something about and has validity over a class of objects. This suggests that a necessary condition, a basic requirement for a philosophical method to be sound is that the philosophical method yields, justifiably, universal knowledge. To understand this basic requirement, we need, first of all, to answer these preliminary questions: Is the universal knowledge philosophy produces of the same kind as the universal knowledge empirical sciences produce? Should we obtain philosophical, universal knowledge in the same way as we obtain scientific, universal knowledge?

In empirical sciences, the natural way to obtain universal knowledge about objects of type X is to collect a group of empirical data about X-type objects, usually through our designing a series of empirical experiments on X-type objects and making empirical observations, and then generalize the empirical data. For example, to obtain the knowledge that bats are blind, we need to do experiments on and observe the behavior of numerous bats, and then generalize. Thus, the universal knowledge empirical sciences produce, the knowledge obtained from empirical generalization in one way or another, can be said to have "empirical universality," according to this definition of "empirical universality": x has empirical universality if and only if (1) x claims or implies that every object of a certain type *is in fact* (or is not in fact) such and such, and (2) x is obtained through empirical generalization, where empirical generalization is not poorly done—that is, it is not inductively weak in an obvious way. For the scientific, universal knowledge is obtained through (inductively strong) empirical generalization, and it claims that every object of a certain type *is in fact* such and such. Can the same thing be said of philosophical, universal knowledge? Is the universality there also the empirical universality?

I don't believe so. Throughout the history of philosophy, it is not a common practice for philosophers to form theses on the basis of empirical generalization. For rationalists, philosophical knowledge is derived from a non-empirical method, for example, recollection of forms, armchair reflection, intuition of essence, and the like. For empiricists, although they claimed that the source of our knowledge is experience, few tried to derive philosophical knowledge on the basis of empirical experimentation and generalization. Many contemporary empiricists used so-called "thought experiments" to derive philosophical knowledge. Yet, in thought experiments, not only do we postulate instead of empirically setting up the circumstances (which are in many cases unreal), but also, the results of thought experiments are obtained from tests of *ourselves only*, not from tests of any other persons or things. In effect, what we do in thought experiments is anything but *obtain data for empirical generalization*, for (1) in thought experiments the obtained data—the test results of *our own reactions*—may not be *empirical* data (and hence, they cannot be used for empirical generalization), and (2) even if they are, the data are simply too restricted to be suitable for empirical generalization.[73] Take Quine's "radical translation" for example.[74] Suppose I want to inquire about the meaning of *Gavagai*. What I do, in the context of radical translation, is to imagine a situation where a native utters *Gavagai* in a certain circumstance, and then watch *my* reaction to the native's utterance by exercising *my* capacities of linguistic understanding, and finally use the observed data to form thesis. Now, what kind of philosophical thesis I can form from the experiment, or whether Quine's thesis is right, is not my concern. My point is this: In the thought experiment of radical translation, we simply *do not* watch the linguists' *actual* practices concerning the interpretation of *Gavagai*, and collect the observed data for empirical generalization and for forming philosophical theory. Instead, we just watch our own reactions to the native's utterance, and use this observation alone to form our theory, where empirical generalization does not take place. Using radical translation as an example, we can clearly see an important feature of thought experiments (which marks an essential difference between thought experiments and empirical experiments): Unlike empirical experiments, thought experiments were not used to produce data for empirical generalization. Thus, philosophical knowledge obtained through thought experiments is essentially different from scientific, universal knowledge, insofar as we do not use empirical generalization to obtain the former. In sum, we have seen that philosophical knowledge in the past was not generally derived from empirical experimentation and generalization, and hence, it did not have empirical universality.

Of course, this does not imply that the universal knowledge philosophy produces does not have empirical universality: We might create new ways of doing philosophy that are different from the way philosophy has traditionally been conducted throughout its history. However, given the close connection between philosophy and the history of philosophy, the above observation does give us a reason to take seriously the claim that philosophical, universal knowledge does not have empirical universality.

This said, let me argue that philosophical, universal knowledge does not have empirical universality. Consider these two examples, in which I try to derive certain philosophical knowledge. Suppose I want to know whether in a single act of perceiving a cube we can see more than three sides of the cube (barring tricky cases). Do I need to present a cube to everyone I know and ask him or her whether he or she sees more than three sides at one time? Of course not. All I need to do is to present the cube to myself, perhaps just once, and then I should be able to answer the question with certainty. Suppose I want to inquire whether we can feel shame without being aware of other's presence. Do I need to do experiments on a group of people (e.g., set up situations that make others feel shame, and ask them whether they are aware of someone else's presence) and then generalize the accumulated data? Of course not. Again, in this case, all I need to do is to run a test on myself. Now, in these two examples, the data I obtain (as a result of the tests on myself) for deriving knowledge are either empirical or non-empirical. If they are non-empirical, of course they cannot be used for empirical generalization. And hence in these examples I do not use empirical generalization. If they are empirical, then if empirical generalization is used, it is inductively weak. Thus, in these examples either I do not use empirical generalization to derive knowledge or I use it poorly. Taking other cases of deriving philosophical knowledge as analogous to these two examples, I claim that philosophical knowledge does not have empirical universality, insofar as it is not obtained through empirical generalization when empirical generalization is not poorly done. As a result, the aforementioned basic requirement for the soundness of a philosophical method now becomes: *The philosophical method yields, justifiably, universal knowledge the universality of which is not empirical universality.* But can universal knowledge have a sort of universality other than empirical universality? What is the other sort of universality if the answer is "yes"?

To answer these questions, let's consider logical inferences. Take, for example, inference of the pattern of *modus ponens*—thinking that if A then B and thinking that A legitimizes thinking that B. Clearly, it is a piece of universal knowledge, because it says something about certain thinking process for all persons and it is valid for everyone. Yet it does not have empirical universality, because (1) it does not mean that for any person X, whenever X thinks that if A then B and that A, she *in fact* thinks that B; and (2) the recognition of such an inference pattern is not made on the basis of empirical generalization, for by observing and generalizing people's *actual* thinking processes we can never sort out any universally held inference pattern, let alone the pattern of *modus ponens*, as at many times people make logical errors or simply think irrationally. Instead, inference of the pattern of *modus ponens* has "normative universality," according to this definition of "normative universality": x has normative universality if and only if (1) x claims or implies that every object of a certain type *ought to be* (or ought not to be) such and such, and (2) x is *not* obtained through empirical generalization. For the inference rule has validity over the thinking processes of all persons, not in the sense that everyone *does* always think in accordance with the rule, but that everyone *should* always think in accordance with the rule; and moreover, it is not formed through empirical generalization. This point is nothing new—philosophers such as Kant, Mill, and Husserl all made similar observations. However, none of them has given us a plausible explanation about how logical inference can have the normativity that they claimed it to have.[75] In other words, they didn't address or satisfactorily answer this question: What kind of method, what sort of epistemic process, can lead us to discover and justify logical inferences as rules with normative universality?

The answer to the above question, I think, lies in pure reflection—it is through pure reflection that we discover and justify logical inferences as normative rules. To discover and justify logical inferences, we need at one stroke to (1) do the logical inferences ourselves, and (2) watch ourselves doing them. Yet, only in pure reflection can we live the reflected-on (e.g., doing the inferences ourselves) and the reflective (e.g., watching ourselves doing the inferences) in a unified way, and only there can we discover and justify the inference rules.[76] But how does pure reflection justify logical inferences as normative rules? Why can it produce universal knowledge with normative universality? To answer them, we must look closely at the structure of pure reflection and the relation between the reflected-on and empirical egos.

First, pure reflection does provide us knowledge. In pure reflection, we achieve a conceptual recognition of the being of the reflected-on (or [most of] the being of the reflected-on*). Because the reflected-on does have a distinct being from the reflective, and because the conceptual recognition is a disclosure of the being of the reflected-on achieved through a reliable method ("a lightning intuition" without taking a point of view), the recognition we obtain in pure reflection is knowledge.

Second, in pure reflection, the reflected-on, the quasi-object for the reflective, is a living consciousness *that is not personal*.[77, 78] We know that the reflective recognizes the non-positional "feel" (of) the reflected-on. But because the non-positional "feel" (of) the reflected-on, as the concrete living being of the reflected-on, involves nothing personal, the recognition we obtain in pure reflection is about an X-ing consciousness, not about an empirical, personal ego.

Note that the reflected-on is neither an abstract idea nor an essence. What happens in pure reflection is radically different from what happens in Locke's "eliminative" sort of abstraction[79] and Husserl's "eidetic variation." According to Locke,

> Ideas become general by separating from them the circumstances of time and place, and any other ideas that may determine them to this or that particular existence. By this way of abstraction they are made capable of representing more individuals than one; each of which, having in it a conformity to that abstract idea, is (as we call it) of that sort.[80]

Thus, when we form the abstract idea of human being, we eliminate the characteristics peculiar to John, Jane, James, and others, and retain only those characteristics common to them all. According to Husserl, "eidetic variation" runs as follows:

> Let us now consider some cases in which a universal is given, i.e., cases where a purely immanent consciousness of the universal is built up on the basis of some "seen" and self-given particular. I have a particular intuition of redness, or rather several such intuitions. I stick strictly to the pure immanence; I am careful to perform the phenomenological reduction. I snip off any further significance of redness, any way in which it may be viewed as something transcendent, e.g., as the redness of a piece of blotting paper / on my table, etc. And now I fully grasp in pure "seeing" the *meaning* of the concept of redness in general, redness *in specie*, the *universal* "seen" as *identical* in this and that. No longer is it the particular as such which is referred to, not this or that red thing, but redness in general.[81]

In both "eliminative" sort of abstraction and eidetic variation, we start with an empirical individual (e.g., a particular object, a particular quality, a person, a personal state, etc.), and then subtract all the empirical character-istics, determinations, and significations of the individual (for Husserl there is an additional step of moving from a non-empirical individual redness to the concept of redness), and finally we "see" the abstract idea or essence as what remains after the subtraction. However, in pure reflection, things are different: We do not start with an empirical individual and then drop its empirical characteristics and determinations; rather, the first, direct object we recognize is a non-empirical, non-personal consciousness, which is absolutely not a production of any sort of abstraction.

In sum, the non-personal reflected-on, the quasi-object for the reflective in pure reflection, is not any of the empirical egos. For an empirical ego, whether it is mine, yours, or other's, is a hypostatized thing-like object (in-itself*), whereas the non-personal reflected-on is not. Moreover, neither is the non-personal reflected-on a form exemplified by empirical egos. For it is not something that is shared by empirical egos (if it were, it would have to contain characteristics that belong to the in-itself). What, then, is the relation between the non-personal reflected-on and an empirical ego?

According to Sartre, my empirical ego is "the projection into the in-itself on the part of the for-itself reflected-on" (EN, 207; BN, 225). That is to say, my empirical ego is the empirical hypostatization of the non-personal reflected-on, in which hypostatization we create a "replica" of the non-personal reflected-on using absolutely different "materials," e.g., the properties and characters that belong to the in-itself. Thus, the non-personal reflected-on both "is" and "is not" my empirical ego. It "is" my empirical ego, in the sense that the non-personal reflected-on serves as the original model for my empirical ego—i.e., *it is an exemplary consciousness that my empirical ego ought to be.* It "is not" my empirical ego, in the sense that the non-personal reflected-on and my empirical ego are beings of two different kinds (i.e., the former is a for-itself, whereas the latter is an in-itself*). Now, because all other empirical egos are hypostatized in a way similar to the hypostatization of my empirical ego, they bear similar relations to the non-personal reflected-on, e.g., *the non-personal reflected-on is an exemplary consciousness that all empirical egos ought to be.*

This said, it is not a big step forward to infer that purely reflective knowledge has normative universality. Take any piece of purely reflective knowledge *a*. Because *a* is about the non-personal reflected-on (i.e., *a* claims that the non-personal reflected-on is [or is not] such and such), and because the non-personal reflected-on is an exemplary consciousness that all empirical egos *ought to be*, it follows that *a* amounts to saying that all empirical egos *ought to be* (or ought not to be) such and such. Moreover, because *a* is not obtained through empirical generalization, *a* is universal knowledge with normative universality. Hence, pure reflection produces universal knowledge whose universality is normative universality.

Contrast pure reflection with empirical generalization. While we use empirical generalization to derive scientific, universal knowledge, the procedure is (or can be) doubly inconclusive: 1. The scope of generalization is confined to the data-sample whereas the knowledge it yields is meant to apply to objects that are not in the sample. In cases where the data for generalization come from empirical experimentation, we cannot be sure that there is a regularity in objects' behavior or the possession of a certain property in the situation we set up, which regularity will go beyond the cases observed—beyond the data-sample. 2. In cases where the data for generalization come from empirical experimentation, we cannot be sure that no hidden elements make the situation we set up for observing the behavior or property of the chosen objects non-standard. However, in pure reflection neither of them applies. "1" does not apply, because we don't perform any sort of generalization in pure reflection, and accordingly we don't have a contrast between the restricted scope of the data-sample and the unrestricted scope of the knowledge based on it. "2" does not apply either, because in pure reflection, the tested subject is the being of the reflected-on*, and there is certainly nothing hidden in the being of the reflected-on*—consciousness is translucent.[82]

Contrast purely reflective knowledge with scientific, universal knowledge. Although they are both universal knowledge, they differ in three important aspects: 1. They have different sorts of universality. Scientific, universal knowledge has empirical universality, whereas purely reflective knowledge has normative universality. 2. They are derived from different epistemic processes. Scientific, universal knowledge is obtained through empirical generalization, whereas purely reflective knowledge is not. 3. They are verified in different ways. To verify scientific, universal knowledge of X-type objects, we need to observe the behavior or property of many Xs, and any unfavorable empirical observation of the behavior or property of a particular X can impose a serious problem. However, to verify purely reflective knowledge, all I need to do is to watch myself living the reflected-on, and the way that any other person in fact is or behaves is not directly relevant to the verification of the knowledge.[83]

Finally, let me point out that purely reflective knowledge has not only normative universality but also "necessity." As I said before, in pure reflection, I live the reflected-on. In doing so, I am a "feel" that I *cannot* live the reflected-on in a way different from the actual way I live the reflected-on, a "feel" that the actual way I live the reflected-on is the *only* way that is permitted by my being (i.e., the totality of my acquired capacities). For example, in making the inference of the pattern *modus ponens*, I am a "feel" that I cannot do the inference differently—i.e., there is no alternative way of doing the inference (e.g., from "if A then B" and

"A" I infer "not B") I am free[84] to choose—this "feel" is missing when I try to do things that I don't know how to do, e.g., Chan meditation. Thus, purely reflective knowledge—the recognition of the reflected-on—is "necessary," in the sense that the being of the reflected-on, as recognized by the reflective, cannot be different from what it is, insofar as I am not free to live the reflected-on differently.

This necessity shouldn't be confused with the necessity of my being. As Sartre pointed out, there is no necessity, no sufficient reason at all, for me to be the being that I am now[85]: I could have lived alone in a desert, practicing yoga, following abrupt instincts instead of logic. But this radical contingency of being does not affect the necessity of purely reflective knowledge, because purely reflective knowledge arises only in the context where my being is already given, determined in one way or another. In other words, of course I could have lived very differently (e.g., I could have been completely irrational); nevertheless, *given my being as I am now*, (barring the brain-malfunction case) while exercising one of my acquired capacities (e.g., the inferential capacity of applying *modus ponens*), I cannot do something arbitrarily (e.g., I cannot infer something other than that B from that if A then B and that A), and hence, what we know in purely reflective knowledge cannot be otherwise. To put in another way, we may view the being we are as a *"framework."* Then the necessity of our being is an *"external"* necessity, the necessity of our "framework" being one way or another. In contrast, the necessity of purely reflective knowledge is an *"internal"* necessity, the necessity manifested in the "feel" (of) the reflected-on *when a framework (my being) is given and is not in question.*[86] Of course, pure reflection by itself is not necessarily a philosophical method, as we have some form of pure reflection in many ordinary non-philosophical activities, e.g., checking proofs, forming and verifying introspective reports, etc. However, the point I hope to have shown is that if a philosophical method includes pure reflection as a component, it then satisfies the aforementioned requirement for the soundness of the method—the requirement that the method produces universal knowledge, the universality of which is not empirical universality.[87, 88]

Conclusion

To recapitulate, I have presented a phenomenological model of Sartre's theory of pure reflection in *Being and Nothingness*. This model should provide us a ground to study the ethical features of pure reflection that Sartre presented in *Notebooks for an Ethics*. Moreover, through elaborating the thesis that in pure reflection we live the reflective consciousness and the consciousness reflected-on* in a unified way, I showed that pure reflection produces knowledge with normative universality. Although pure reflection is not by itself a developed philosophical method, a philosophical method including pure reflection as a component satisfies a basic requirement for any sound philosophical method, the requirement that the philosophical method produces universal knowledge, the universality of which is not empirical universality.

Notes

1. In *The Transcendence of the Ego*, an analog of the notion of "pure reflection" is the notion of "non-thetic memory" (or "non-reflective memory"). (See note 38 for further discussions.) See TL, 30–32; TE, 46–48.

2. Thomas Anderson claimed that the ontological descriptions of consciousness Sartre gave in *Being and Nothingness* were made on the level of impure reflection rather than on the level of pure reflection (Anderson, *Sartre's Two Ethics*, 54). I disagree. For Sartre said in *Being and Nothingness, part two, chapter two, section III* that his purpose of discussing pure reflection was to justify the ontological descriptions of consciousness (EN, 197; BN, 212), which suggests that the ontological descriptions were made on the level of pure reflection.

3. Note that although all properties of being-in-itself (e.g., the three properties of being-in-itself that Sartre mentioned in *section VI* of *Introduction* to *Being and Nothingness*) are uncovered in our investigation of the phenomenon of being rather than in pure reflection (EN, 30; BN, 24–25), the *existence* of being-in-itself is proved by appealing to the general structure of consciousness as manifested in pure reflection (EN, 27–29, 220–28; BN, 21–24, 240–49).

4. To my knowledge, only two authors—Kathleen Wider and Thomas Busch—gave a serious discussion of pure reflection as an important methodological concept. See Wider, *Bodily Nature*, 74–85; Thomas Busch, "Sartre's Use of the Reduction: *Being and Nothingness* Reconsidered," in *Jean-Paul Sartre: Contemporary Approaches to his Philosophy*, ed. Hugh Silverman and Frederick Elliston (Pittsburgh: Duquesne University Press, 1980), 17–29. As I will argue, both of their accounts are flawed, and my account of pure reflection is different from theirs.

5. Besides the phenomenological *epoché*, there are two other methodological

movements in Husserl's phenomenology: the eidetic seeing and the theory of constitution. These three movements are distinct and yet interwoven.

6.   I say roughly, because (1) "pure reflection" is the central notion in Sartre's methodology, whereas the phenomenological *epoché* is just one part of the phenomenological method, and (2) pure reflection has ethical implications, whereas the phenomenological *epoché* does not.

7.   Busch, for example, claimed that pure reflection is just the phenomenological *epoché* as applied to consciousness itself. See Busch, *The Power of Consciousness and the Forms of Circumstances in Sartre's Philosophy* (Bloomington, Ind.: Indiana University Press, 1990), 33; Busch, "Sartre's Use of the Reduction," 25.

8.   In this paper, Husserl's *epoché* is treated only as a leading thread to Sartre's pure reflection, so my discussion of Husserl is brief and sketchy. Moreover, because of the space constraint, I will not explain some of Husserl's notions that I introduce, if they are well known.

9.   An intentional object is transcendent if and only if it is not immanent.

10.   See Husserl, *The Idea of Phenomenology*, 6, 28.

11.   Husserl, *The Idea of Phenomenology*, 6, 27.

12.   Husserl, *Ideas*, 79.

13.   Note that (3) is *not* a variant way of stating (2). For belonging to the same conscious stream that includes consciousness X is different from being contained in X. Suppose I am recalling my perception of an airplane yesterday. The perception I am recalling is not a part of my current recalling consciousness, because the perception existed in the past (yesterday) and no longer exists. However, the perception belongs to the same conscious stream that includes my current recalling consciousness, because they are both mine. Thus, according to (3) the perception *is* an immanent object, whereas according to (2) the perception *is not*.

14.   E.g., for the rejection of (1), see Husserl, *Ideas*, 78–80; Husserl, *Cartesian Meditations*, 25–26; Husserl, "Phenomenology" (for the *Encyclopaedia Britannica*), in *Husserl, Shorter Works*, ed. Peter McCormick and Frederick Elliston (Notre Dame, Ind.: University of Notre Dame Press, 1981), 24–25; for the rejection of (2), see Husserl, *Ideas*, 78–80.

15.   Husserl's passing discussion of "perception of something immanent" in *Ideas* is similar to some of what Sartre said about pure reflection, when Husserl said that "[i]n the case of a perception directed to something immanent, or briefly expressed, *a perception of something immanent* (so-called 'internal' perception), *perception and perceived* form *essentially an unmediated unity, that of a single concrete cogitatio*" (Husserl, *Ideas*, 79–80). However, as we shall see, without Sartre's notion of "non-positional consciousness" (which is missing in Husserl's system), we lack the essential tool to make sense of the unity between the perceiving and the perceived in Husserl's "perception of something immanent."

16.   Following Sartre, I use 'unreflected consciousness' to designate the being

of consciousness rather than an idea of consciousness posited in certain reflection. By "unreflective consciousness," I mean an unreflected consciousness whose intentional object is not consciousness.

17. See Husserl, *Ideas*, 179; Husserl, *Cartesian Meditations*, 27–28.

18. Husserl, *Cartesian Meditations*, 37, 49.

19. Husserl, *Ideas*, 179.

20. It is not clear how Husserl *can* know anything about the unreflected mental processes. If what Husserl said concerning the unreflected mental processes is evidentially grounded, it must be made in an appropriate reflection. But in that reflection how can the intentional object be the actual reflected consciousness rather than a reconstructed counterpart?

21. See Husserl, *Ideas*, 75, 87–88, 236–40.

22. See Husserl, *Cartesian Meditations*, 17–18.

23. See Husserl, *Cartesian Meditations*, 17–18.

24. Some philosophers such as John Austin think that such a consciousness does not exist (if 'corrigible' is taken in the philosophical sense). For even in the immediate introspection there could be misuses of words in the language to report the momentary experience.

25. Not all philosophers agree on this. Those who reduce a *cogitatio* to a physical or dispositional state or event deny the epistemological privilege of immediate introspection.

26. There is no evidence that Husserl held *only* the weak version. However, the weak version is a more common-sensical understanding of the adumbration thesis.

27. Note that the weak version works best with perception by sight and touch, but less so (or it does not work at all) with perception by hearing, smell, and taste. I owe this observation to Paul Spade.

28. Of course, we can do so only if we assume the stability of the world, e.g., the sides I saw and touched before are still there when I see and touch the other sides. However, it could be argued that this stability can be assumed, insofar as there is no *real* violation to this stability.

29. Note that even at this stage my consciousness can still be subject to errors from illusion.

30. Husserl, *Cartesian Meditations*, 61–62.

31. Husserl, *Cartesian Meditations*, 62.

32. Sartre called this "the principle of series" (EN, 12–14; BN, 5–7).

33. Note that these are exactly some of the key moves in Husserl's theory of constitution. Thus, the strong version of the adumbration thesis is closely related to Husserl's constitution theory.

34. Note that unlike errors from illusion, whose scope covers the whole realm of consciousness of something transcendent, errors from adumbration (whether of the weak or strong version) are found in only perceptual consciousness.

35. I will discuss Sartre's sense of "apodictic evidence" later. But let me point

out here that Sartre didn't worry about errors from illusion, and he rejected the strong version of the adumbration thesis in *Being and Nothingness* (EN, 27–29; BN, 21–23).

36. My notion of "reflective" is the same as Sartre's notion of "reflective" (EN, 197; BN, 212).

37. What I mean by "reflected-on" is what Sartre meant by "unmodified reflected-on" in the context of pure reflection (EN, 199; BN, 215), and what he meant by "in-itself-shadow of the reflected-on" in the context of "impure reflection" (EN, 207; BN, 214–15). I will discuss "impure reflection" and "in-itself-shadow of the reflected-on" later.

38. This example of watching myself writing was introduced by Sartre in *The Transcendence of the Ego* to illustrate "non-thetic memory" (TL, 30–31; TE, 46–47), and a different version of the example was introduced in *Being and Nothingness* to illustrate pure reflection (EN, 198; BN, 214). Given that Sartre's discussions of the example and the different version of the example are remarkably similar in the two places, it is reasonable to extrapolate that "non-thetic memory" in *The Transcendence of the Ego* is an analog of "pure reflection" in *Being and Nothingness*.

39. Here, I don't mean that checking a logical proof involves nothing but pure reflection. In fact, it involves some extra part that is clearly *not* pure reflection—i.e., comparing my inference with the objective rule. However, my point is that checking a logical proof does involve pure reflection.

40. What I mean by "reflected-on*" is what Sartre meant by "reflected-on" (EN, 196–209; BN, 212–226).

41. This may look odd at first sight, but if we consider it carefully, there does not seem to be any problem with it—it is simply a peculiar feature of pure reflection. In particular, there is no bad faith involved in pure reflection, because in it we omit rather than purposefully deny the "existing-for-a-witness-feel"(of) the reflected-on*.

42. In a section on reflection in *The Bodily Nature of Consciousness*, Kathleen Wider seemed to think that the non-positional consciousness (of) pure reflection is different from the non-positional consciousness (of) the reflective and the non-positional consciousness (of) the reflected-on* (Wider, *Bodily Nature*, 76). But in his discussion of the non-positional "feel" (of) pure reflection Sartre never took it as something separate and different from the "feels" (of) the reflective and the reflected-on* (EN, 198–99; BN, 214–15). Because Wider chose as her focus the non-positional consciousness (of) pure reflection in separation from the non-positional consciousnesses (of) the reflective and the reflected-on*, she paid little attention to the unity of the reflective and the reflected-on* in her study on pure reflection.

43. "The reflected-on has then, in a way, already a consciousness (of) itself as having *an outside* or rather the suggestion of *an outside*" (EN, 199; BN, 214).

44. "[I]t [the reflective] is profoundly affected in its being by its reflectivity

and consequently can never achieve the *Selbständigkeit* at which it aims, since it derives its being from its function and its function from the for-itself reflected-on" (EN, 199; BN, 214).

45. According to Sartre, the dyad refers to the two sides of our consciousness: The term 'reflection' in the dyad "reflection-reflecting" refers to the positional consciousness (acquaintance), and the term 'reflecting' refers to the non-positional consciousness ("feel") (EN, 118; BN, 122). Note that "reflection-reflecting" in this sense does *not* mean "reflection" and "reflecting" in the sense we have just been talking about (whether in pure reflection or not). These (*reflet-reflétant*) are different expressions in French.

46. With respect to the reflected-on*, the subject matter is usually worldly objects, whereas with respect to the reflective it is the reflected-on.

47. "Reflection, as the mode of being of the for-itself, must be as temporalization, and it is itself its past and its future. . . . The reflective is not the apprehension of an instantaneous reflected-on, but neither is it itself instantaneity. This does not mean that the reflective knows *with* its future the future of the reflected-on and *with* its past the past of the consciousness to be known. On the contrary it is by means of the future and the past that the reflective and the reflected-on are distinguished within the unity of their being. The future of the reflective, in fact, is the ensemble of its own possibilities which the reflective has to be qua reflective. As such it could not include a consciousness of the future reflected-on" (EN, 203; BN, 220).

48. What this implies is that in pure reflection both the reflective and the reflected-on* are not instantaneous—they are rather processes.

49. "Proper subclass" because there are many acquaintances, e.g., emotional consciousness, actional consciousness, that are not knowledge*.

50. Note that 'taking a point of view' can have a narrow and a broad sense. In the narrow sense, it just means taking a cognitive position on physical objects (or imagined physical objects). In the broad sense it means taking a cognitive perspective on any object, whether physical or not. For example, in the broad sense, we say that we take a point of view on the essence of an equilateral triangle by thinking of the equality of its three angles. Hereafter I use the term in the broad sense.

51. Note that this is an example of knowledge* of a physical object, not an example of reflection. But what I say concerning this example applies to all knowledge*, including a certain bad sort of reflection ("impure reflection").

52. In Sartre's words, pure reflection is "a lightening intuition without relief, without point of departure, and without point of arrival" (EN, 202; BN, 218).

53. If someone insists on keeping the "point-of-view" talk, she can at most say that we obtain pure reflective recognition by taking *the* point of view, because the relation between the reflected-on and the reflective cannot be otherwise.

54. According to Sartre in *The Psychology of Imagination*, in a perception (1) it is risky (i.e., liable to error) to posit the intentional object and (2) the object is

given in profiles (PI, 9–10).

55. According to Sartre in *The Psychology of Imagination*, in an imagination (1) it is not risky to posit the intentional object and (2) the object is given in profiles (PI, 11–12).

56. According to Sartre in *The Psychology of Imagination*, in a conception (1) it is not risky to posit the intentional object and (2) the object is not given in profiles (PI, 9–10).

57. For Sartre, the knowledge* we obtain in conception is incomplete, as he said that our grasp of the essence of a cube "need[s] to complete itself by an infinite progression" (PI, 10) and that "[e]ven mathematical essences are revealed to us with an orientation in relation to other truths, to certain consequences; they are never disclosed with all their characteristics at once" (EN, 202; BN, 218–19). Here Sartre's points are these: 1. In conception, the intentional object is essence. 2. An essence is uncovered in perspectives, where a perspective is a particular way to grasp the essence *in relation to other essences*. 3. An essence cannot be uncovered completely, because an essence can bear infinite relations to infinite other essences, i.e., there are infinite perspectives from which to grasp the essence.

58. Strictly speaking, it is the "Me," not the "I," that is constituted in *The Transcendence of the Ego*. I realize that Sartre's terminology was not always consistent there, but when he was being careful in *The Transcendence of the Ego*, the "I" is the transcendental ego (which he of course rejected entirely), whereas the "Me" is the *psyche*. And it is the *latter* that he was describing the constitution of in *part II* of *The Transcendence of the Ego*. He gradually changed his terminology in *The Transcendence of the Ego*, and by the end of it, the "I" is the *active* side of the psyche, while the "Me" is the *passive* side.

59. In *The Transcendence of the Ego*, the "I" or "Me" is constituted from one of three directions: (1) from momentary experience to the constitution of states and then to the constitution of qualities and then to the constitution of the Ego, (2) from momentary experience to the constitution of states and then to the constitution of the Ego (omitting qualities), and (3) from momentary experience to the constitution of actions and then to the constitution of the Ego (TL, 44–74; TE, 60–93). As a result of the constitution, the Ego appears as the transcendent pole from which all its states, qualities, and actions are emanated—the direction of emanation is just the opposite of the direction of constitution. In *Being and Nothingness*, although it is debatable whether Sartre still accepted his earlier Husserlian theory of constitution, he clearly held the same views concerning the emanation relations among the Ego, its qualities, states, and actions (EN, 209–10; BN, 226–27).

60. The "if. . ." part is obvious. The "only if. . ." part holds because (1) "the necessary and constant correlate of impure reflection" is "the shadow of the reflected-on" (I will discuss the notion of "shadow" later) (EN, 208; BN, 226), (2) the unity of those shadows of the reflected-on "is called the *psychic life* of *psyche*" (EN, 208–9; BN, 226), and (3) "[b]y Psyche we understand the Ego, its states, its qualities, and its acts" (EN, 209; BN, 226).

61. For Sartre, the agent's acts include both physical actions (e.g., playing a piano, driving a car) and mental actions (e.g., doubting, making a hypothesis, constituting objects from sense data) (TL, 51–52; TE, 68–69). A definition of "acts" is given as follows: "By *acts* we must understand the whole synthetic activity of the person; that is, every disposition of means as related to ends, not as the for-itself is its own possibilities but as the act represents a transcendent psychic synthesis which the for-itself must live" (EN, 210; BN, 227).

62. Another way to identify impure reflection is that, in impure reflection, we posit either (1) the interrelations among psychic states, qualities, and actions (or the momentary experience [*Erlebnis*]) (e.g., "my humiliation of yesterday is the total motive for my mood this morning" [EN, 216; BN, 234]) or (2) the causal relations between the psychic states, qualities, or actions (or momentary experience) on the one hand and the in-itself on the other (e.g., the antipathy that I feel toward a person is the reason why I do not go to that person's house [EN, 218; BN, 237]), and yet in either case the posited relations do not really exist in the original consciousness, before it was reflected on (EN, 215–18; BN, 233–37).

63. Note that Husserl's phenomenological *epoché* leads us ultimately to impure reflection, since the realm it opens for us—consciousness as a combination of the hyletic material, the synthesizing principle, and the transcendental ego—is nothing but an in-itself* version of the consciousness reflected-on*.

64. Note that an intentional object is magical if and only if it has both the character of the in-itself and the character of the for-itself at the acquaintance side (TL, 61; TE, 78–79).

65. In *The Transcendence of the Ego* Sartre didn't actually use the term 'apodictic evidence'; he used the term 'adequate evidence' (TL, 48; TE, 64).

66. Note that in this sense not all knowledge* lacks apodictic evidence. Mathematical knowledge* or any knowledge* that neither is nor is based on perception has apodictic evidence.

67. I say "most" because in certain impure reflection whose posited object is not manifested in profiles, e.g., an impure reflection in which we posit the momentary experience or the synthesizing principle, errors from adumbration are not found.

68. For example, according to Sartre in *The Transcendence of the Ego*, my having the experience of repugnance for Peter is not adequate to posit my hatred for Peter (TL, 45–49; TE, 62–65).

69. "Reflection—if it is to be apodictic evidence—demands that the reflective *be* that which is reflected-on" (EN, 198; BN, 213).

70. Although Sartre referred to the "ideal form" of reflection (i.e., pure reflection) in discussing the motivation for reflection (EN, 201; BN, 218), Sartre later told us that impure reflection shares with pure reflection the same sort of motivation: The motivation for impure reflection "is within it in the twofold movement, which we have already described, of interiorization and of objectivation: to apprehend the reflected-on as in-itself in order to make itself be that in-itself

which is apprehended" (EN, 207; BN, 224).

71. "Reflection is a second effort [the first effort is manifested in the reflection-reflecting dyad] by the for-itself to found itself; that is, *to be for itself what it is*" (EN, 200; BN, 216).

72. This section is a further development of Sartre's theory of pure reflection that I presented in the previous section. The views I propose here, e.g., that pure reflection produces knowledge that has normative universality, were not explicitly held by Sartre, but they seem to follow from his theory of pure reflection.

73. Of course, to say that the data we obtain in thought experiments are unsuitable for empirical generalization does not necessarily imply that it is impossible for us to use the data for empirical generalization. However, if we were to do so, thought experiment would become an obviously bad way to derive universal knowledge.

74. W. V. Quine, *Word and Object* (Cambridge: Technology Press of MIT, 1960), *Chapter II.*

75. Husserl, for example, had a theory of intuition of the "ideal" to account for the universality of logical rules (Husserl, *Logical Investigations*, trans. by J. N. Findlay [London, Routledge and Kagan Paul, New York: Humanities Press, 1970], *Prolegomena to Pure Logic*). But it is not clear how exactly his "visionary" theory works.

76. Note that, in pure reflection, there are two ways to formulate our discovery of logical inferences: the "objective" way, paying more attention to the positional side of consciousness, which gives us, in the case of *modus ponens*, that if A then B and that A implies that B; and the "subjective" way, paying more attention to the non-positional side of consciousness, which gives us, in the case of *modus ponens*, that thinking that if A then B and thinking that A legitimatizes thinking that B. These two formulations are different descriptions of the same thing, and they are both right if we understand them in the correct context—the context of describing a consciousness that is doing logical inferences.

77. In *The Transcendence of the Ego*, for example, Sartre argued that the transcendental consciousness is not personal (TL, 19–23; TE, 37–40).

78. In terms of this thesis we escape solipsism. However, a further objection might be raised: Although the reflected-on is not recognized as a personal ego in pure reflection, after all, the reflected-on is included as a part of the reflected-on* that belongs to my empirical ego, and hence, isn't our theory a version of methodological solipsism? My answer is "no," for the claim that the reflected-on* belongs to my empirical ego is and can only be made in *impure* reflection.

79. The "eliminative" sort is one of the two sorts of abstraction proposed in Locke's *An Essay Concerning Human Understanding*. The other one is the "accretive" sort, according to which we form abstract ideas by accreting determinates of particulars. Both accounts run together in his famous triangularity example.

80. John Locke, *An Essay Concerning Human Understanding*, 3, 3, 6.

81. Husserl, *The Idea of Phenomenology*, 44–45.

82. Perhaps an example will help illustrate the differences between empirical generalization and pure reflection. Suppose we want to inquire what we feel while we peep through a keyhole and hear a footstep behind. In the way empirical psychology approaches it, we need to perform experiments on different persons and then generalize—particularly, first, we need to set up the appropriate situation, e.g., asking different persons (which may or may not include myself) to peep through the keyhole and creating the sound of a footstep, then we observe the reactions of those tested persons in the situation, and finally we generalize. Now, in this procedure we see two limitations: First, the persons we experiment on are finite, and we cannot be sure that there is a regularity in persons' reactions to the situation beyond the cases observed. Second, we cannot be sure that there is no unintended hidden element in the situation to which the tested persons may have reacted (unless we ask the tested persons what elements in the situation they are reacting to). In pure reflection, however, things are different: First, I don't perform experiment on different persons—the only person involved is myself, and the knowledge is formed on the basis of self-observation alone. Second, in watching myself reacting to the situation, I am quite sure about what I am aware of and what I am reacting to. Thus, in pure reflection we don't have the above two limitations.

83. For example, with respect to the verification of the inference rule *modus ponens*, an empirical observation that a person X does not think in accordance with the rule at a particular time is incapable of falsifying the rule.

84. In this paragraph I use 'free' in the ordinary sense, not in the Sartrean sense.

85. The view of radical contingency of our being is compatible with the evolutionary account of mankind. If we hold the latter, we shall readily admit that purely reflective knowledge is different in different eras, as people acquire new capacities and lose old ones from time to time. However, the procedure of pure reflection remains the same.

86. Here I use the terms 'framework', 'external', and 'internal' to suggest a possible connection with Carnap's views on analyticity and his distinction between things "external" and "internal" to the linguistic framework (Rudolf Carnap, "Empiricism, Semantics, and Ontology," in *Semantics and the Philosophy of Language*, ed. Leonard Linsky [Urbana, Ill.: University of Illinois Press, 1952], 209–11).

87. Note that this is not as strong as the claim that any philosophical method including pure reflection as a component is sound. It is beyond the scope of this chapter to argue for or against this strong claim.

88. Note that a philosophical method including impure reflection as a component does not satisfy this requirement. In impure reflection, the reflected-on is *stipulated* rather than *lived* by ourselves. Thus, impure reflection does not produce *knowledge*. Hence, impure reflection does not produce universal knowledge, the universality of which is not empirical universality.

Chapter Six

Authenticity I: Do We Abandon the Project of Trying To Be God in Authenticity?

Introduction

Whereas the notion of "bad faith" remains stable in Sartre's early philosophy, the notion of "pure reflection" and "good faith" undergo changes in the period from *Being and Nothingness* to *Notebooks for an Ethics*. In *Being and Nothingness*, pure reflection was presented as a necessary but not sufficient condition for authenticity[1], whereas in *Notebooks for an Ethics*, 'pure reflection' and 'authenticity' seemed to refer to the same consciousness (although with different emphasis[2]) (NE, 12, 472–82; 515).[3] In *Being and Nothingness*, the project of good faith was introduced as a corrupted mode of being, which, like bad faith, stands in contrast to authenticity (EN, 108–11; BN, 113–16), whereas in *Notebooks for an Ethics*, Sartre did not seem to distinguish good faith from authenticity (NE, 12).

Among the secondary literature, a popular interpretation[4]—most notably Thomas Anderson's—is that Sartre's authenticity involves an particular kind of *ontological* conversion: a conversion from a project of trying to be God to a project that does not involve trying to be God at any level—a project of trying to be freedom. On the basis of this ontological conversion, it claims, we can subsequently have an *ethical* conversion: a conversion from a project that takes God as the ultimate value to a project takes freedom as the ultimate value.

In this chapter I argue against this popular interpretation. I argue that contrary to the popular view, in authenticity we do *not* abandon the project of trying to be God. Through a close look at Sartre's discussion of "play"

in *Being and Nothingness*, I offer a theory of authenticity or pure reflec-
tion*; this theory will be developed further in the next chapter by consulting the *Notebooks for an Ethics*.

Criticism of Anderson's Account

One of the main theses in Thomas Anderson's *Sartre's Two Ethics* is that
we reject the project of trying to be God in authenticity. There is no doubt
that this thesis fits well with Sartre's general project of founding ethics on
the basis of ontology. Nonetheless, it has an obvious problem: Because it
rejects the inclusion of the project of trying to be God in authenticity, it has
to downplay or find a way to qualify a well-known claim in *Being and
Nothingness*—that the project of trying to be God is *inevitable*. How did
Anderson do that? And did he succeed?

Anderson qualified the above claim (that the project of trying to be God
is inevitable) by qualifying the entire ontology in *Being and Nothingness*.
Anderson recognized that Sartre defined human beings as projects of trying
to be God in *Being and Nothingness*. However, he claimed that although
the structure of trying to be God is inevitable in the ontology developed in
Being and Nothingness, it is not inevitable without qualification. According
to him, the entire ontology in *Being and Nothingness* is to be rejected in
authenticity. He said:

> *Being and Nothingness* made little mention of this distinction [the
> distinction between pure and impure reflection], and, when it did, it stated
> that it was going to leave the discussion of pure reflection or conversion
> for ethics. In fact, Sartre stated explicitly in *Being and Nothingness* that
> he was dealing there only with descriptions on the level of impure, or
> accessory, reflection. I might add that recognition of this is crucial for a
> proper interpretation of much of that ontology, for it means that it
> generally describes human reality, its relation to others and to the world,
> from the perspective of impure reflection (or sometimes simply on the pre-
> reflective level) but not from the perspective of pure reflection or
> conversion. Sartre affirms this when he asserts, on the fourth page of his
> *Notebooks*, "*Being and Nothingness* is an ontology before conversion!"[5]

Anderson thought that the ontology in *Being and Nothingness* is to be
rejected in authenticity because *Being and Nothingness* "generally
describes human reality, its relation to others and to the world, from the

perspective of impure reflection. . . but not from the perspective of pure reflection or conversion." To justify the latter, he partly relied on the claim that "Sartre stated explicitly in *Being and Nothingness* that he was dealing there only with descriptions on the level of impure, or accessory, reflection." However, this claim is imprecise. The references Anderson gave to support the claim are two: one in the context of the discussion of reflection in general (EN, 207; BN, 224), the other in the passage where Sartre discussed "play" (EN, 670; BN, 742). However, the former contains no allusion at all to Anderson's claim that the ontological descriptions in *Being and Nothingness* are made on the level of impure reflection. In the latter, Sartre said that study of "the particular type of project which has freedom for its foundation and its goal." "belongs rather to an *Ethics* and it supposes that there has been a preliminary definition of nature and the role of purifying reflection (our descriptions have hitherto aimed only at accessory reflection)" (EN, 670; BN, 742). I suspect that it is the sentence in parentheses that led Anderson to claim that the ontological descriptions in *Being and Nothingness* were made on the level of impure reflection. However, if we read this sentence carefully in its context, we find that all Sartre was saying is that we have described only (the nature and the role of) accessory or impure reflection. It is one thing to say that we have *described* only impure reflection, and it is quite another thing to say that what we have described (the ontology in *Being and Nothingness*) *was made on the level of* impure reflection.[6]

Moreover, not only is it imprecise to say that Sartre claimed in *Being and Nothingness* he was dealing only with descriptions on the level of impure reflection, but also, Anderson's claim that *Being and Nothingness* generally described human reality from the perspective of impure reflection (or sometimes simply on the prereflective level) is false. First, the claim is ambiguous. It could mean that *Being and Nothingness* described only unreflective consciousness and impure reflection. Or it could mean that in *Being and Nothingness* the ontological descriptions of consciousness were made *through* impure reflection. Yet, in both cases, the claim is false. In the first case, it is false because *Being and Nothingness* also described the ontological characteristics of pure reflection. In fact, Sartre spent a whole section in *Being and Nothingness*—*section III* in *chapter two* of *part two* of *Being and Nothingness*—discussing the ontological characteristics of pure reflection, including the ontological difference between pure and impure reflection. And that section is the *only* place in Sartre's early works that contains a detailed discussion of the ontological characteristics of pure reflection. Thus, contrary to Anderson's claim that *"Being and Nothingness* makes little mention to the distinction between pure and impure reflection, and when it does, it states that it is going to leave the discussion of pure reflection for ethics,"[7] *Being and Nothingness* does contain a detailed discussion of pure reflection.[8] In the second case, it is false because Sartre stressed several times that the ontological descriptions of consciousness are made through *pure reflection*. In effect, Sartre spent an entire section on pure reflection (*section III* in *chapter two* of *part two* of *Being and Nothingness*); in that section, he tried to convince us that all the ontological descriptions of consciousness he gave in *Being and Nothingness* were made, justifiably, through pure reflection.

Finally, there is a general difficulty associated with Anderson's rejection of the entire ontology of *Being and Nothingness* in authenticity. If the entire ontology in *Being and Nothingness* is to be rejected, exactly on *what ground* should Sartre's ethical theory be based? We know that Sartre tried to build his ethics on the basis of ontology. We also know that there is nowhere in Sartre's early works that he developed an alternative ontology. Thus, when Sartre developed his ethical theory in *Notebooks for an Ethics*, he had to use at least part of the ontology presented in *Being and Nothingness* as his basis. Hence, the ontology in *Being and Nothingness* cannot be rejected entirely in building a positive ethics.

In sum, Anderson did not convincingly show us that the ontology in *Being and Nothingness* can be qualified in the way he did. Thus, Anderson's strategy of qualifying the claim that the God-project is inevitable in terms of qualifying the ontology in *Being and Nothingness* does not work. Consequently, he is not successful in establishing that we reject the project of trying to be God in authenticity.

Rejection of the God-project in Authenticity?

This said, let me argue that Sartre's radical conversion does not involve the rejection of the God-project. I shall first show that the *Conclusion* of *Being and Nothingness* leaves open the question whether authenticity involves the rejection of the God-project.

There are very few places[9] in *Being and Nothingness* where Sartre discussed ethics. *Section II* of the *Conclusion* is one of those few places. In that section, after claiming that, in the project of trying to be God, we have a natural tendency to take God as the ultimate value, Sartre said:

But hitherto although possibles could be chosen and rejected *ad libitum*, the theme which made the unity of all choices of possibles was the value or the ideal presence of the *ens causa sui* [= "the being that is the cause of itself" = God]. What will become of freedom if it turns its back upon this value? Will freedom carry this value [that is, the in-itself-for-itself] along with it whatever it does and even in its very turning back upon the in-itself-for-itself? Will freedom be reapprehended from behind by the value which it wishes to contemplate? Or will freedom, by the very fact that apprehends itself as a freedom in relation to itself, be able to put an end to the reign of this value? In particular is it possible for freedom *to take itself* for a value as the source of all value, or must it necessarily be defined in relation to a transcendent value which haunts it? And in case it could will itself as its own possible and its determining value, what would this mean? (EN, 722; BN, 797-798.)

This freedom [the new ultimate value] chooses then not to *recover* itself but to flee itself, not to coincide with itself but to be always at a distance *from* itself (EN, 722; BN, 798).[10]

In the above passages it is clear that Sartre inquired about the possibility of rejecting God as the ultimate value and was considering a possibility of replacing God with freedom. Note here that the phrase 'God as the ultimate value' has two different senses in *Being and Nothingness*.[11]

In the first, it is understood as an *ontological* doctrine, as the claim that we are non-positionally aware that we always make ourselves to be God. In this sense, the God-value is not to be interpreted as an ordinary value that is grasped *positionally*, but as an essential goal *at the side of the non-positional consciousness*. In other words, the God-value is not a positional correlate of our desiring or willing, but a characterization of the importance of the goal in the structure of the non-positional consciousness. For example, when I work as a cashier unreflectively, I seek God as the ultimate value, in the sense that my non-positional consciousness (of) making myself to be a cashier has its goal as the Cashier-God. The Cashier-God or any other social-position-God has value not because it is desired or willed (that is, we have the non-positional consciousness [of] desiring or willing. . .), but because it is an essential part (the goal) of the non-positional consciousness (of) trying to be God. When Sartre discussed the God-value in *chapter one* of *part two* ("Immediate Structure of the For-Itself") of *Being and Nothingness*, he was referring to this first sense.

In the second sense 'God as the ultimate value' is understood as an *ethical* doctrine, as the claim that we ultimately desire or will God. In this sense the God-value is like an ethical value, which is grasped positionally, as the positional correlate of desiring or willing. Note that the second sense is *different* from the first. For in working as a cashier unreflectively, I must seek for God (Cashier-God) as the ultimate value in the first sense, but I *do not have to* seek for God as the ultimate value in the second sense.

When Sartre discussed the God-value in the final pages of *Being and Nothingness*, he was taking it in the second sense, for two reasons. First, these final pages are in the section entitled "Ethical Implications." Second, in those final pages Sartre claimed that in the project of trying to be God, we have a natural tendency to take God as the ultimate value. If 'God as the ultimate value' is taken in the first sense, Sartre should not say that we *have a natural tendency* to take God as the ultimate value in trying to be God—it is simply an analytic truth that we take God as the ultimate value in trying to be God.[12] Thus, the authenticity or conversion that Sartre considered in the final pages is solely an *ethical* conversion—the replacement of the ultimate *ethical* value. Moreover, Sartre neither said nor hinted there that the *ethical* conversion requires an *ontological* conversion in the sense Anderson proposed—the replacement of the God-project with some other project that does not involve trying to be God at any level. In sum, *section II of the Conclusion of Being and Nothingness* leaves open the question whether we need to jettison the project of trying to be God in authenticity.

This said, I shall propose an account of what Sartre possibly had in mind in the final pages of *Being and Nothingness*. Let me start with an analogy from sports.[13]

Suppose I am a runner, and I compete in a marathon race. While I am running the race, all I want is to win it. Indeed, winning is the ultimate goal and value to which everything else is subordinated.[14]

But now suppose I start to think differently. I treat racing as something subordinate to a *different and higher* value. Racing is no longer just to win the game. It is for the sake of something else, e.g., to cultivate the spirit of competition, etc. So now, winning is no longer the ultimate value. It is replaced by a new one. With this new attitude, although I don't stop trying any less to win, whether I do win in the race doesn't really matter. Even if I lose the race, or even if winning is strictly impossible, I may still attain the higher goal of cultivating the spirit of competition.

So perhaps the final pages of *Being and Nothingness* suggest an account of authenticity similar to the (oversimplified) marathon analogy. In authenticity, we don't stop trying to be God, and we cannot stop trying to be God. Thus, the whole ontological structure developed through *Being and Nothingness* is intact. However, in authenticity we come to view the value of being God as *subordinate* to some higher value—the freedom. We may never achieve the lesser value (being God), but in the process of trying to be God I may very well succeed in achieving the new and higher value (freedom). According to this account, radical conversion does involve an ethical conversion: replacing the old value (being God) with the new one (freedom). But it does not involve the rejection of the project of trying to be God.

To see whether this account is a plausible way to understand authenticity, let's take a close look at Sartre's discussion of "play."

Play

In *Being and Nothingness*, play was introduced as a peculiar type of project that has freedom as its foundation and its goal, as contrasted with "the spirit of seriousness" (EN, 669–70; BN, 740–41). A connection between play and authenticity is hinted in the following passage from *Being and Nothingness*:

> The first principle of play is man himself; through it he escapes his natural nature; he himself sets the value and rules for his acts and consents to play only according to the rules which he himself has established and defined. As a result, there is in a sense "little reality" in the world. . . . [In play,] [t]he act is not its own goal for itself, neither does its explicit end represents its goal and its profound meaning; but the function of the act is to make manifest and to present to *itself* the absolute freedom which is the very being of the person. This particular type of object, which has freedom for its foundation and its goal, deserves a special study. It is radically different from all others in that it aims at radically different type of being. It would be necessary to explain in full detail its relations with the project of being-God, which has appeared to us as the deep-seated structure of human reality. But such a study can not [cannot] be made here; it belongs rather to an *Ethics* and it supposes that there has been a preliminary definition of nature and the role of purifying reflection (our descriptions have hitherto aimed only at *accessory* reflection); it supposes in addition taking a position which can be *moral* only in the face of values which haunt the For-itself (EN, 669–70; BN, 741–42).

It seems from the above passage that play serves as a prototype of authenticity in *Being and Nothingness*, insofar as it does not involve the spirit of seriousness; it makes manifest freedom; and it is closely related to purifying or non-accessory reflection.

In the first place, play is directly opposed to the spirit of seriousness. A person with the spirit of seriousness "considers values as transcendent givens independent of human subjectivity" (EN, 721; BN, 796), "transfers the quality of 'desirable' from the ontological structure of things to their simple material constitution" (EN, 721; BN, 796), and hence attributes "more reality to the world than to oneself" (EN, 669; BN, 741). In short, the spirit of seriousness is in bad faith—it hides one's freedom at the positional side and it understands and values oneself as a transcendent object among others. For example, working as a waiter in the unreflective state does not commit oneself to the spirit of seriousness, but justifying one's action (to work as a waiter) by defining oneself as the social position "waiter" (as one thing being another) does involve the spirit of seriousness. However, in play there is little reality in the world, i.e., one does not value the rules and regulations that she consents to follow more than she values the subjectivity of herself. When we play hide-and-seek, there are certainly rules to follow in order to play the game. However, in playing we are the non-positional "feel" that the rules *are not* something we *have to* follow, something that is more important than ourselves. Rather, the rules are something we choose and something we consent to follow.

Second, play makes manifest freedom. This does not mean just that the non-positional "feel" (of) play is spontaneous or is free in the technical sense we espoused in chapter 3. Rather, it means that, in play, we are the non-positional "feel" that we are not restrained by any "have-to." In play, we do not have to win. We do not have to follow the rules and regulations. We can quit at any time. In short, in play, we do only things that we feel comfortable doing.

Third, play can easily lead to pure reflection. Although in play we do have a goal to achieve (e.g., winning a game), it is the nature of the project of play that we are the "feel" that the achievement of the goal is not the only thing that matters to us. This "feel" can easily lead to the awakening (reflective) consciousness that the achievement of the goal does not have the ultimate value, that it has value only in the context that we consent to play, that there are other things that have values too. This awakening consciousness involves at least part of pure reflection, because it brings to light the subjectivity and freedom in our choosing to play.

In play, we do not stop trying to be God. We follow rules and regulations; we have a goal (e.g., winning the game) to achieve. This confirms the account suggested in the previous section, that in authenticity we do not reject the project of trying to be God.

Although in play we still try to be God, we do not play just to achieve a certain goal. Rather, we play *for fun*—joyful experience that does not come just from the realization of the God-project. The fun we seek in play certainly includes the pleasure derived from our achieving a chosen goal in play, but it is more than that, because it is common sense that we enjoy *playing* at least as much as we enjoy achieving the chosen goal in play. Let's look closely at the fun we seek in play.

First, the fun includes *the enjoyment of novelty* (which appeared in the process and as a result of play), an unpredictable result that we help create in play. In playing cards, it is the uncertainty of my possession of the cards, the uncertainty of others' possessions of the cards, and the uncertainty of the proceedings of each hand that are always fascinating. In playing tennis, it is the unforeseeable trajectory of the ball that makes the game fun to play. Moreover, the enjoyment of the novelty in play is not derived from our merely observing and contemplating the uncertainties; it is rather derived from our working with them in a certain way. In other words, to have the enjoyment of the novelty in play, not only do we need a novel result, but also, we need to (1) care about the result, (2) not care too much about the result, and (3) help create the result. If we don't care about the result at all, the novelty manifested in the result will not be so fascinating and intriguing. When I merely watch a certain person playing cards with others, the others' possession of cards is certainly a novelty to me, but it is not as intriguing to me as it is when I participate in the game. If we care too much about the result, the novelty will appear to be frightening rather than intriguing. If I spend all my savings on a certain game in a casino, the result of the game is frightening instead of intriguing. If we do not help create the novelty, the novelty will appear as an unexpected surprise rather than an anticipated fascination. If I receive (regular) mail on holidays, I am surprised but not fascinated.

Second, the fun includes the excitement derived from the achievement of the goal (e.g., winning the game) in play. Note that the achievement of the goal can bring excitement *only if it appears as a novelty that we help create in the context of play*. If the achievement of the goal is guaranteed, there is simply nothing exciting in achieving the goal. For a prince, there is little fun in playing competitive games, because the victory is predetermined.

Third, the fun includes the relaxing "feel" that we are free from any transcendent constrains. As I said before, there is no "have-to" in play. I play in exactly the way that I feel most comfortable to play. In switching to the attitude of "play," I am the "feel" that all obligations, all authorities, all transcendent values are gone all at once and that I am free to do exactly what my mind and body want me to do concerning the way to play. Such a "feel" (of) removal of all constrains is most relaxing, and it constitutes the fun in play.

In the above, I have offered an account of play, which confirms the suggestion that in authenticity we do not reject the God-project, given the close relation between play and authenticity. Play is not limited to those consciousnesses that engage in ordinary games. We can transform any project-related consciousness into play. All we need to do is to insert the playful attitude and let it take over all other attitudes. We can play in trivial projects such as driving to a supermarket—for example, we can play to try a totally new route. We can play in important projects such as teaching a course—for example, we can play to change teaching strategies in every week.

Conclusion

In conclusion, according to my interpretation, in authenticity we do not cease trying to be God. We cannot. However, in authenticity the God-project serves a higher purpose — it serves to achieve freedom: we live the God-project only insofar as we recognize and will the God-project in pure reflection, and with the realization that we must inevitably fail at being God. Sartre's radical conversion is certainly an ethical conversion; it is a process of reorientation of ethical values. But it is not an ontological conversion in the sense that Anderson proposed.

Notes

1.   "But such a study [of the particular type of project which has freedom for its foundation and its goal] can not [cannot] be made here; it belongs rather to an *Ethics* and it supposes that there has been a preliminary definition of nature and the role of purifying reflection. . . ; it supposes in addition taking a position which can be *moral* only in the face of values which haunt the For-itself" (EN, 670; BN, 742). This passage seems to suggest that pure reflection is a necessary but not sufficient

condition for authenticity.

2. To emphasize the contrast with unreflective consciousness and bad faith, Sartre used the term 'authenticity'; to emphasize the contrast with impure reflection, Sartre used the term 'pure reflection'.

3. In the following let me use 'pure reflection' for the notion of "pure reflection" that Sartre presented in *Being and Nothingness, part two, chapter two, section III*, 'pure reflection*' for the notion of "pure reflection" that Sartre presented in *Notebooks for an Ethics*.

4. E.g., see Anderson, *Sartre's Two Ethics*, chapter 4; Santoni, *Bad Faith*, chapter 7.

5. Anderson, *Sartre's Two Ethics*, 54.

6. It is perfectly possible that all ontological descriptions in *Being and Nothingness* are made on the level of pure reflection and that we described only impure reflection.

7. I suspect what Anderson had in mind is only one paragraph in Sartre's discussion of "play," where the name 'purifying reflection' is mentioned once (EN, 670; BN, 742).

8. EN, 670; BN, 742.

9. E.g., the famous footnote on authenticity, the discussion of "play," *Section II* of the *Conclusion*.

10. This new value of not being self-identical was also suggested in Sartre's "Existentialism Is a Humanism," where Sartre took freedom as the great value—not God. It is the prototype of "authenticity" or "pure reflection*" in *Notebooks for an Ethics*. (In *Notebooks for an Ethics*, Sartre seems to treat 'pure reflection' and 'authenticity' as being synonymous. E.g., see NE, 12, 472–82, 515.)

11. So far, no commentators have distinguished these two senses.

12. Following Sartre's remarks in the end of *Being and Nothingness*, hereafter I take 'God-value' in the second sense.

13. I borrowed the idea of sport analogy from Paul Spade.

14. This is similar to what we have seen in *Being and Nothingness*.

Chapter Seven

Authenticity II: Reconstructing the Childish Heart

Introduction

In the previous chapter, I discussed play as a prototype of authenticity. Whereas play is unreflective, authenticity is reflective. In this chapter, I carry further the study of authenticity by interpreting authenticity as a reflective consciousness modeling after certain features in play. Through examining three ethical features of authenticity or pure reflection* that Sartre presented in *Notebooks for an Ethics*, I show that a fundamental attitude underlies authenticity, a passion to reconstruct the childish heart.

Two Criticisms

Before we start to work out Sartre's theory of authenticity in detail, let's first address two well-known criticisms: 1. Sartre's theory of authenticity does not provide us an ethics, because it is a choice to be non-ethical.[1] 2. Sartre's theory of authenticity does not teach us anything significantly new, in spite of the novel terminologies it used. Authenticity amounts to nothing than more than the reflective awareness of freedom and the realization of ordinary wisdom that we should value the process more than the result.

In some cases, the critics try to make a case for the claim that the choice of authenticity is non-ethical on the basis of two premises: 1. In authenticity Sartre placed the ultimate value at the "immediate self-realization" of our being. 2. The choice to value the "immediate self-realization" of our being is a non-ethical choice.

To understand the two premises, we need to understand a distinction between the immediate self-realization and the temporal self-realization[2]. The immediate self-realization is the aspect of ourselves in which we simply act out of the instantaneous desire or random whim without any consideration of our temporality.[3] The temporal self-realization is the aspect of ourselves in which we assume the responsibility of our past and future, i.e., to let our current action be bound by past resolution and to let our current resolution bind our future action.[4]

As Barnes pointed out, premise 2 is problematic.[5] For the valuing of the immediate self-realization can spring from either a non-ethical choice or an ethical choice.[6] In the case of Dostoevski's Underground Man, the choice to value the immediate self-realization is a non-ethical choice. However, the valuing of the immediate self-realization can also spring from an ethical choice, e.g., a choice based upon our reflectively weighing the pros and cons of the immediate self-realization and those of the temporal self-realization.

Not only is premise 2 problematic, but also premise 1. How do the critics justify the premise 1? Normally the critics appealed to one of these two reasons: (1) Sartre placed the ultimate value at the spontaneity of freedom, and the spontaneity of freedom is just the randomness of the instantaneous whim; (2) in Sartre's theory there is no room for the temporal aspect of the self, insofar as the self as a substance persisting throughout time is merely a constituted, magical object. To the first reason, one may respond that the critics wrongly conflate the spontaneity of freedom with the randomness of the instantaneous whim. Although the spontaneity of freedom is manifested in the instantaneous whim, it also is manifested in any consciousness that involves temporal self-realization. It might be tempting to use the common understanding of the randomness in the instantaneous whim to demystify Sartre's technical sense of the spontaneity of freedom. But they are not exactly the same thing.

The second reason might seem to be appealing at first sight. In *Transcendence of the Ego*, Sartre discusses how we constitute the ordinary notion of the temporal self. In *section III, chapter two, part two* of *Being and Nothingness* Sartre makes the further claims that the ordinary notion of the temporal self is constituted in *impure reflection* and that it should be purged in pure reflection. Now, because there is no room for the temporal self-realization in authenticity, there must be room for its opposite—the immediate self-realization (for one can argue that there is not much left of our life besides these two sorts of self-realization). More important, Sartre's denial of the temporal self could support the claim that the choice to be authentic is a non-ethical choice through a different, more direct argument. For any ethics uses and is based upon the notion of the temporal self. Without the notion of the temporal self, we cannot have any motivation to control and to justify ourselves. And without such a motivation, we cannot have any ethics. Are these views tenable?

I agree that Sartre takes the ordinary notion of self as a constituted psyche to be rejected in authenticity. However, I disagree that Sartre has no notion of the temporal self. According to my reading, Sartre does have an account of the temporal self. For him the temporal self is nothing other than the current non-positional consciousness as being essentially connected to the past and future non-positional consciousnesses. Here the connections are not based on a prior unity of the self as an identical substance. Rather, the connections are non-reducible, essential components of the current non-positional consciousness. It is in remembrance that we are connected to the past non-positional consciousness. Along with the non-positional feel (of) the homogeneity of the past non-positional consciousness and the current non-positional consciousness, I apprehend the past non-positional consciousness as *my* past by willing to be responsible for the remembered decisions and actions. In other words, we are infected but not affected with the remembered non-positional consciousness. We are not affected with the remembered non-positional consciousness, because (1) the spontaneity of the remembered non-positional consciousness is contingent upon the spontaneity of the remembering, and (2) the hedonistic material of the remembered non-positional consciousness is gone. In this sense, the remembered non-positional consciousness is the *past*. Yet we are infected with the remembered non-positional consciousness, because in remembering, our current non-positional consciousness is "melting into" the remembered non-positional consciousness. In this sense, the remembered non-positional consciousness is *my* past.

The connection to the future non-positional consciousness is more complicated. On the one hand, I am connected to the future in the way of (1) anticipating the future non-positional consciousness and (2) making a deferred willing. First, it is a fact that we can anticipate the future non-positional consciousness. I know that the anticipated non-positional consciousness is *my* non-positional consciousness, because I expect that the current non-positional consciousness will turn into the anticipated non-positional consciousness. Second, I can issue a will with deferred binding force—a deferred willing because (1) in remembrance, I feel that I am tied to my past (my past action, my past willing, etc.) and (2) I take my relation to the anticipated future as just the reverse of my relation to the remembered past. On the other hand, I feel that I am bound by the past deferred willing in remembrance. When the deferred willing matures, it turns into a binding willing here and now. But this is possible only because (1) I remember the willing as *my* willing and (2) I remember the willing as a *deferred* willing, which was supposed to turn into an effective willing in the future. If it is in connection with anticipation that the deferred willing comes into being, it is through remembrance that the deferred willing is put into work.

Using the above connections as irreducible primitives, it is fairly easy to develop a notion of temporal self. The self is simply the current non-positional consciousness along with the connected past and future non-positional consciousnesses. Even if we drop the notion of the temporal self, by using the connections as primitives, we still can make sense of the ethical notions such as "responsibility" and "self-control."

In the above I answered the first criticism. In order to answer the second criticism, we need to work out the ethical features of authenticity.

The First Feature of Authenticity: Willing to Will What We Will

It is often claimed that pure reflection* or authenticity, as Sartre presented it in *Notebooks for an Ethics*, is simply a reflective awareness of one's freedom. If this claim is right, how can it be the case that authenticity gives value to freedom whereas non-positional "feel" in an unreflective consciousness does not, although they are both consciousness of (or [of]) one's freedom? To answer this question, and to determine whether authenticity is just a reflective awareness of one's freedom, let's take a close look at the notion of "pure reflection*" in Sartre's *Notebooks for an Ethics*.

Unlike the notion of "pure reflection" in *Being and Nothingness*, the notion of "pure reflection*" or "authenticity" in *Notebooks for an Ethics* was introduced with three ethical features. The first ethical feature it has is that in authenticity we will or issue a consent to the project reflected-on. In *Notebooks for an Ethics*, Sartre said:

... reflection is not contemplation. It is a form of willing. If the project is not recaptured contemplatively, at least it is recaptured *practically*. Reflection makes this project one's *own*, not through identification or appropriation but by consent and forming a covenant. . . . Pure, authentic reflection is a willing of what I will. It is the refusal to define myself by what I am (Ego) but instead by what I will (that is, by my very undertaking, not insofar as it appears to others—objective—but insofar as it turns its subjective face toward me) (NE, 479).

When we are engaged in a project unreflectively, of course we will what we will in the project, because we are busying ourselves with the object that we will in the project and we are non-positionally aware (of) the project. What we will in the unreflective project is a certain object in the world. However, in purely reflecting* on the same project (i.e., living the project in authenticity), things are different: Not only do we will the object that we do in the original unreflective project, we also will the very project itself, not as something posited by others or as an impurely reflective consciousness, but as an ongoing process happening here and now. For example, suppose I am participating in a tennis match, and am trying very hard to win the game. In the game, what I will is my victory. However, when I purely reflect* on my participating in the match (i.e., participating in the match in authenticity), I add an extra thing as an object of my willing: my playing the match. Here, at the level of pure reflection* or authenticity, it is no longer the objective victory that has the ultimate value. Rather, it is the prosecution of the project—my playing the match—that has the ultimate value. In other words, when I participate in the match in authenticity, although I still will the victory, the victory is only the secondary object of my willing: What I primarily will is my playing the match. But because in my playing the match, I will my victory, I also will the victory as the secondary object. The situation here is similar to play. In play, the achievement of the goal does not have the ultimate value, and it has value only in the context that it occurs as a novelty. Similarly, in authenticity, the fulfillment of the goal in the unreflective project does not have the ultimate value, and it has value only in the context that we will the unreflective project. In sum, the first ethical feature of authenticity or pure reflection* is that in authenticity there is a willing of the unreflective project; in other words, we will to will what we will. How can authenticity have such a feature?

In *Notebooks*, Sartre suggested that the reason is that we recognize in authenticity that the unreflective project is contingent, and that it is *necessary* that this project is contingent. In *Notebook II*, Sartre said:

[C]onsciousness, if it stops deploring its underlying structure, will be able to attain its necessity within its gratuitousness. It is not necessary that it should exist, but it is necessary that this not be necessary; it is not necessary that it should have just this point of view, but it is necessary that it have some point of view and that this point of view is not necessary (NE, 491).

Because it is necessary that the project is contingent, we transform the contingency of the project into *an absolute freedom*—freedom because the project is contingent and *absolute* freedom because the contingency of the project is necessary, and thereupon we take up the project as ours with a passion. Hence, we will the unreflective project in authenticity.

If we consider the above reasoning carefully, it seems to be flawed. First of all, it is problematic that we will X if X is necessary. But even if we grant that we will X if X is necessary, *note here X is a property of the project—the contingency of the project—not the project itself.* In other words, even if we grant that we will X if X is necessary, all we can say here is that we will the *contingency* of the project (which means, we may will *any* project, not necessarily the unreflective project in question, insofar as every project we freely choose is contingent), but not that we will the *project* that we are currently engaged in.

It is interesting to compare Sartre's authenticity with Kierkegaard's "knight of infinite resignation." Like the authentic person who recognizes the futility of the God project, the knight of infinite resignation also recognizes the absurdity of the project, and yet he does not give up the project. However, the detailed paths for holding on an absurd project are different in their theories. Sartre's approach is rational, whereas Kierkegaard's approach is irrational. Sartre appealed to reason to justify our willing the unreflective project, whereas Kierkegaard appealed to emotion as the source to override the rational/ethical control. Sartre's authentic person is serene and contemplative, whereas Kierkegaard's knight of infinite resignation is turbulent and mad.[7]

To sum up, in authenticity we will to will what we will. Authenticity is not just a counterpart of non-positional consciousness at the reflective plane. Although authenticity and non-positional consciousness both involve an awareness of (or [of]) one's freedom, authenticity—unlike non-positional consciousness—contains something more. Authenticity contains, at the reflective plane, a willing of my participating in the unreflective project, which explains why authenticity values freedom (contingent project) whereas non-positional consciousness does not. Hence, the claim that authenticity is just a reflective awareness of one's freedom is not exactly right: Authenticity contains a reflective awareness of one's freedom, but it is more than that.

The Second Feature of Authenticity: Joy

In *Notebook II,* Sartre said that authenticity is "a double source of joy: through the transformation of gratuity into absolute freedom—through the contact with the being of the phenomenon" (NE, 491). How exactly should we understand that?

In the last chapter, I discussed the joy in play. The joy in authenticity is analogous to the joy in play, insofar as the joy in authenticity, like the joy in play, is a joy of certain novelty we help to create. The novelty in authenticity is manifest at two places: the subjective side of my unreflective project (my non-positional "feel" [of] the project) and the objective side of my unreflective project (the things that I am positionally aware of in the unreflective project).

The novelty at the subjective side of my unreflective project appears in connection with the first source of joy in authenticity, the transformation of gratuitousness into absolute freedom. When I transform the gratuitousness of unreflective consciousness into absolute freedom, that is, when I recognize that the contingency of the unreflective project is necessary, I realize that the subjective part of my unreflective project is full of novelty. At every moment the progress of the unreflective project appears to me as something new, something undermined and unpredictable.[8] The novelty here is somewhat different from the novelty in play: Whereas the novelty in play is manifest both in the result of a project the I freely choose (e.g., who wins the card game) and in the process as what appears at the objective side (e.g., the possession of my cards), the novelty in authenticity (in the subjective part of my unreflective project) is manifest only in the process of the unreflective project as the non-positional "feel" (of) the unreflective *project* (e.g., the way I play cards).

The novelty at the objective side of the unreflective project appears in connection with the second source of joy in authenticity, the contact with the being of the phenomenon (the in-itself). In authenticity, what appears at the objective side—the disclosure on the basis of the for-itself's contact with the being of the phenomenon—is undermined and unpredictable at every moment in the unreflective project. Hence, it manifests a sort of novelty. Like the novelty in play, the novelty here is intriguing because (1) we care about the disclosure of the being of the phenomenon, (2) we don't care too much about the disclosure of the being and the phenomenon, and (3) we help create the novelty.

We care about the disclosure of the being of the phenomenon because (1) the disclosure of the being of the phenomenon is important to our unreflective project (the fulfillment of the goal in the project is marked by a certain disclosure of the being of the phenomenon) and (2) the disclosure of the being of the phenomenon is "absolutely valid"—"absolutely valid" in the sense that there is no other source (e.g., God)[9] to falsify a disclosure than through another disclosure or set of disclosures. This rules out idealism, because if idealism is right, we will not care about the disclosure of the being of the phenomenon (the disclosure of the being of the phenomenon is no longer a "disclosure"). As Sartre put it, "in idealism, it [consciousness] loses all joy because it and the world appear as pure relativity" (NE, 496).

We do not care too much about the disclosure of the being of the phenomenon because (1) the achievement of the goal in the unreflective project does not have the ultimate value and (2) every disclosure of the being of the phenomenon is falsifiable in principle by another disclosure or set of disclosures.

We help create the disclosure of the being of the phenomenon because we choose the unreflective project and we partly determine what we see in the chosen unreflective project. This rules out realism, because if realism is right—we are just passive observers—we then play no role in the disclosure of the being of the phenomenon. As Sartre put it, "in realism, consciousness loses all joy by becoming pure contemplative passivity, epiphenomenal" (NE, 496).

In the above, I have shown that there is a novelty (at the subjective side and at the objective side) as there is in play. However, the novelty by itself—although intriguing (with respect to the novelty at the objective side)—still cannot bring joy. The novelty can bring joy *only in the context of our willing the unreflective project*. It is because we will to will what we will—we have a passion for the unreflective project—that we enjoy the novelty in authenticity.

Although the joy in authenticity and the joy in play do not have exactly the same source, the joy in authenticity can be viewed as a reflective analog of the joy in play. The joy in play is an unreflective enjoyment whose object includes the novelty derived from transcendent beings and which takes place only in the context of our freely choosing a project and determining the rules and regulations of the project. The joy in authenticity is a reflective enjoyment whose object is the novelty derived from the reflective awareness of the contingency of the unreflective project and the awareness of the disclosure of the being of the phenomenon, and which takes place only in the context of our willing and taking up the unreflective project at the reflective level.

To sum up, we have seen that the joy in authenticity, like the joy in play, is directed toward a certain novelty. We have also seen that the joy in authenticity cannot appear in a purely contemplative project (a reflective project of merely contemplating the unreflective project). It is in the context of our willing the unreflective project that the novelty brings enjoyment.

The Third Feature of Authenticity: Authentic Love for Others

The third ethical feature that authenticity has is that in authenticity we have "authentic love for others." To understand the "authentic love for others," we need to first clarify the notions of (transcendental) "self" and "other minds."

In *The Transcendence of the Ego*, Sartre approached the problem of other minds in the context of criticism of solipsism. The problem he tried to solve is this: How can I be sure that there are other consciousnesses?

This problem arises because I assign different status to my Ego and to other's Ego. I have a special access to my Ego in a way that I lack to other's Ego. And that special access gives me a sort of infallibility about my own case that I cannot have when I talk about other's Ego.

While most people tried to solve the above problem by working out some way to allow us to be sure about other's Egos as we are about our own, Sartre went the other way around. Instead of trying to raise our knowledge of other Egos to the level of our knowledge of our own, he lowered the knowledge of our own Ego to the level of our knowledge of other Egos. According to him, I don't have any sort of special access to my Ego that I don't have to anyone else's. Since my Ego and other's Ego are both objects for consciousness, I can be mistaken about my Ego just as much as I can about other's Ego. Thus, all Egos are of the same status. There is no disparity between my Ego and other's Ego. Hence, the problem of other minds is solved.

In *Being and Nothingness*, Sartre came to think that his earlier solution of the problem of other minds is unsatisfactory. He said:

> Formerly I believe that I could escape solipsism by refuting Husserl's concept transcendental "Ego." At that time I thought that since I had emptied my consciousness of its subject, nothing remained there which was privileged as compared to the Other. But actually although I am still persuaded that the hypothesis of a transcendental subject is useless and disastrous, abandoning it does not help one bit to solve the question of the existence of Others (EN, 290–91; BN, 318).

Why did Sartre think that his earlier solution does not work? Obviously, if the problem is how I can be sure that there are other consciousnesses, and if consciousness is understood as Ego (an object for consciousness), his solution in *The Transcendence of Ego* does work. The reason, it seems to me, is that in *Being and Nothingness* Sartre had a different understanding of consciousness and that, with the different understanding, he had a different problem. There Sartre understood consciousness as the being of consciousness, not as *some constituted object for consciousness*, such as the Ego. So the problem of other minds that Sartre tried to solve in *Being and Nothingness* is this: How can I be sure that there is the being of other consciousness like the being of my own consciousness?

This time, Sartre solved the problem in a different way. He didn't argue that I do not have a special access to the being of my own consciousness. In fact I do. I have a special access to the being of my consciousness through non-positional consciousness. Rather, he argued that I, too, have a special access to the being of other consciousness through non-positional consciousness. In fact my being have a dimension of "being-for-others," as reflected in the non-positional "feel" (of) shame, being looked at, etc. In other ways, the very being of my consciousness (e.g., the non-positional "feel" [of] shame) presupposes the existence of the being of other consciousness.

This account has several problems. First, in this account the being of other consciousness thus presupposed is not a flesh and blood human being. It is merely Other Subjectivity. Second, nothing in this account shows there are more than one other consciousnesses. Third, the argument that is used to show that the being of my consciousness presupposes the beings of other consciousnesses has some unwelcome results. Consider the peeping-Tom example. I am peeping through a keyhole and I hear footsteps. I immediately feel shame. Because shame is shame in the presence of other consciousness, the non-positional "feel" (of) shame presupposes the being of other consciousness. It is no doubt true that in this example the being of other consciousness is presupposed by the shame consciousness. However, several other things are presupposed as well, e.g., that the being of other consciousness has a body, that the footstep is an indication of the bodily movement of other consciousness. In short, the example that shows there is no disparity between the existence of my consciousness and the existence of other consciousness also shows that there is no disparity between the existence of my consciousness and the existence of body and no disparity between the existence of my consciousness and the common facts about body. But it seems to me that Sartre would not welcome the thought that the common facts about body (which is integrated with the common knowledge of causality) have the same status as the facts about the being of my consciousness.

Even if Sartre's theory of other minds has problems, one might think that his theory of (transcendental) self is problem free if we can accept his theory of non-positional consciousness, insofar as Sartre told us many times that non-positional consciousness is *self-consciousness*.[10] This thought might be appealing at first sight. However, if we consider it carefully, we find that we need to answer the following question before we can accept the above thought: How and why is non-positional consciousness *self-consciousness*?

To the view that non-positional consciousness is self-consciousness, one can raise the following criticism: The view that non-positional consciousness is self-consciousness has the implication that we are non-positionally aware (of) the non-positional consciousness, for if non-positional consciousness is consciousness (of) something other than consciousness itself, it cannot be called self-consciousness. But this implication is problematic because it introduces infinite non-positional consciousnesses (of different levels) into one single consciousness. Take any consciousness X. We know that we are non-positionally aware (of) our positional awareness. Call this non-positional consciousness "the level 1 non-positional consciousness." Now, in order to be non-positionally aware (of) the level 1 non-positional consciousness, we need another positional consciousness to do the job. Call this non-positional consciousness (of) the level 1 non-positional consciousness "the level 2 non-positional consciousness." For similar reasons, we need the level 3 non-positional consciousness, the level 4 non-positional consciousness . . . in a single consciousness.

But that seems implausible, because it is not clear how we can have infinite non-positional consciousnesses in a single consciousness. Hence, we cannot be non-positionally aware (of) the non-positional consciousness, and accordingly, non-positional consciousness is not self-consciousness. Is this criticism tenable?

I don't think so.

In the above criticism, there is an assumption that a non-positional consciousness is not non-positionally aware (of) itself. However, in my "present-tense-feel" account of non-positional consciousness, this assumption is false. As I said in chapter 1, a non-positional "feel" is none of "the way to feel," "the thing felt," and "the totality of the way to feel and the thing felt." In a non-positional "feel" we cannot separate the being of a "feel" ("the way to feel") from what the "feel" is the "feel" (of) ("the thing felt"). Rather, a "feel" is at the same time a felt-feeling and a feeling-felt. In other words, the non-positional "feel" (of) a "feel" X (i.e., "the way to feel") is included in the "feel" X. Thus, a non-positional consciousness is non-positionally aware (of) itself. Accordingly, there is no higher level of non-positional consciousnesses in a consciousness, and hence the above criticism does not work.

This said, let me point out that the self can be accounted for by non-positional consciousness in two ways. First, we can develop an account of self by appealing to the present non-positional consciousness, together with its connection with the past and future non-positional consciousnesses, as we did in Section 1. Second, we can develop an attribute-based theory of self. We can use the common attribute of non-positional consciousness, the attribute of being self-conscious, the "feel" (of) intended-intending, to account for the self.

The above accounts of the self have the following implications. First, in either account of the self, death should not be a serious concern. Whether or not the self is the present non-positional consciousness or the "feel" (of) intended-intending, it makes no good sense to worry about the death of self. For it is the very nature of our consciousness that we have no absolute control over the future non-positional consciousness—we can expect and work toward the non-positional consciousness at the next moment, but there is no absolute guarantee that we will be it until the moment we are it. Now, if death is the termination of the future non-positional consciousness, it is something we face at every moment as soon as we are born, for at every moment there is a possibility that we will not be at the next moment. But because we do not worry about the future non-positional consciousness being gratuitous, the fear of death is disarmed. Second, in either account of the self, we see that the self, like the other mind that Sartre tried to derive in the being of consciousness, is not personal. The self is not a flesh and blood human being; it is highly "abstract," as Thomas Anderson said.[11]

Have discussed Sartre's theory of self and other minds, let me look at the "authentic love for others." In *Notebook II* Sartre explained an original structure of "authentic love for others" as follows:

> Here is an original structure of authentic love (we shall have to describe many other such structures): to unveil the Other's being-within-the-world, to take up this unveiling, and to set this Being within the absolute; to *rejoice* in it without appropriating it; to give it safety in terms of my freedom, and to surpass it only in the direction of the Other's ends. (NE, 508)

Perhaps we can illustrate Sartre's points through an example. Suppose I see a person climbing up a tree while I am reading. In an unauthentic state, I turn that person into an object, for example, an organism that has all the relevant physical properties, a nuisance if the sound made by her climbing interrupts my reading. However, in authenticity, not only do I observe the physical properties of the person and the objective relation between her and the tree ("to unveil the Other's being-within-the-world"), but also, I grasp and deeply appreciate her *freedom*: I observe that she is engaged in a project of climbing up the tree that she freely chooses. On the ground of the disclosure of her physical properties and the properties of the tree, I note her contingency (the gratuitousness of her project of climbing the tree), her finitude (the coefficient of adversity she encounters, e.g., the height of the tree, the gravity, etc.), her fragility (the possibility of her falling down), and her ignorance (the aspect of reality relevant to her project that she is ignorant of, e.g., the branch she is stepping out has deep fissures ["to take up this unveiling (of the Other's being-within-the-world)"]). I also note that it is necessary that her project is contingent ("to set this Being within the absolute"). I then show a great passion, an authentic love for her freedom and the project she freely chooses, not because her project will be beneficial or in any way related to my project, but because I extend the willing of my freedom, my project to the willing of her freedom, her project.[12] As Sartre put it, I *"rejoice* in it [other's freedom] without appropriating it," and I "give it safety in terms of my freedom" (NE, 508). Finally, I apprehend her project in terms of my knowledge about her and the surrounding environment, which usually does not coincide with her apprehension of her project ("to surpass it only in the direction of the Other's ends").

One noteworthy feature of Sartre's "authentic love for others" is that authentic love for others arises in a context where nothing more than contemplation is needed. In an authentic relation with others, it seems that we do not have to take the place of others in their projects, nor do we have to actually do anything to help others' realizing their projects. What we need to do, it seems, is just step back and watch, showing love for others' freedoms and projects but without doing anything, and having satisfaction in watching. Such an authentic relation with others, if practiced across the board, seems to lead to an individualistic, cold, and helpless world.

Reviving the Childish Heart

In the above, we have discussed three ethical features of authenticity. We have seen that the second feature of authenticity—joy—presupposes the first feature (willing of the unreflective project), insofar as the novelty in authenticity brings joy only in the context of our willing the unreflective project. We have also seen that the third feature of authenticity—authentic love for others—presupposes the first feature too, insofar as in authentic love for others, I extend the willing of my unreflective project to the willing of other's project. However, we haven't found a way to justify the first feature. How can we will the unreflective project in authenticity?

The answer, it seems to me, is that in authenticity we have a passion to revive the childish heart, a passion to play and to explore new experience. In a child's eye, process is more important than result, and value is found in the living of the project-related consciousness rather than in the realm of things. It is through our reviving the childish heart that we gain the justification to will the unreflective project in authenticity.

To revive the child's heart does not mean to fall back to live as a child in the original state. It rather means to recreate the child's perspective at a new level using pure reflection as a guard. When a child grows older, it is natural that the child's perspective is gradually replaced by the attitude of seriousness. In other words, the child's perspective in its original state (as in the child) is vulnerable to the attitude of seriousness. However, when we revive or recover the child's perspective in authenticity, the *recovered* child's perspective can withstand the attitude of seriousness. Because the perspective is recovered through pure reflection, and pure reflection overturns the legitimacy of the attitude of seriousness. In this sense, the recovered child's perspective is an ethically sophisticated perspective.

The passion to revive the childish heart is incompatible with bad faith. The passion to revive the childish heart occurs in connection with pure reflection—it is because of pure reflection that the revival could overturn the attitude of seriousness. But with pure reflection, with recognition of the non-positional consciousness (of) the project-related consciousness, the lie in bad faith collapses, and bad faith becomes cynicism.

The passion we discuss here is similar to the passion that Buddhists have for consciously (reflectively) living every moment in awakening. In awakening, a Buddhist turns an ordinary consciousness extraordinary—she relives the ordinary consciousness with a passion for the living experience of every moment in the consciousness and without attaching to the common values in the consciousness. Although in Buddhism, we don't have an developed account of non-positional consciousness and pure reflection, the living experience of which Buddhism makes a great deal is analogous to non-positional consciousness.

Like the Buddhist's passion in awakening, the passion in authenticity presupposes the devaluation of the empirical self (the Ego) in relation to the non-positional "feels" (living experience in Buddhism). In Buddhism, if we keep the empirical self as the center of our attention, as we normally do in either self-indulgence or self-denial, we would not take notice of and have a passion for the living experience. Similarly, in authenticity if we value the empirical self more than the non-positional "feels," we would certainly value the goals and aims that empirical self desires in God-projects. In that case, we would value the God-projects more than the non-positional "feels," instead of the other way around.

Although the passion in authenticity and the Buddhist's passion in awakening both presuppose the devaluation of the empirical self, the devaluation is held for different reasons. In Buddhism, there are various reason for the devaluation of the empirical self, but the main reason is this: It is the empirical self that is essentially related to all sorts of "suffering" (the gap between the world as we desire and the world as we in fact have) and Buddhism aims to terminate "suffering" for good. In authenticity, however, we devalue the empirical self in relation to the non-positional "feels" because (1) through pure reflection we know that the non-positional "feels" characterize the real being of consciousness, (2) we value something that is real more than something that is not real, and (3) the empirical self is not real—through pure reflection we know that the empirical self is not a genuine component of our consciousness.[13]

In the above, I have sketched an account that interpreted authenticity as a reflective transformation of play. Now it should be noted that authenticity cannot be a prevailing attitude across the board in ordinary life. If one adopts a playful attitude (whether unreflectively or reflectively) across the board all the time, it is quite likely that she will lose all her securities and that she cannot satisfy her basic needs. If I play at my job all the time, the result of my work is at best unstable, which is likely cause me to lose my job. If I play at my marriage, I will ruin the relation with my spouse—my playful attitude will deeply hurt the feelings of my spouse. If I play at my friendship, I will lose most of my friends—I will be too capricious to be trusted by my friends. In short, the adoption of the playful attitude across the board is unfeasible in practical life, because it is quite likely to make us lose securities (e.g., job) and to dissatisfy our basic needs (e.g., need for friendship).

Conclusion

In the above, I have discussed three ethical features of authenticity that Sartre presented in *Notebooks for an Ethics*. I have argued that the second feature (joy) and the third feature (authentic love for others) presupposes the first feature (willing to will what we will) and that, underlying the first feature, is a fundamental passion of reviving the childish heart. To see whether and how these ethical features link to the ontological characteristics of consciousness, let's move to the next chapter.

Notes

1. For a discussion of the first criticism, see Hazel Barnes, *An Existentialist Ethics* (New York: Alfred A Knopf, 1967), part 1, chapter 1.

2. Barnes introduced and discussed this distinction in *An Existentialist Ethics*, 16–19.

3. In the way that Barnes puts it, the immediate self-realization is a consciousness that wills "itself nontemporal to the extent of refusing to make remembrance or anticipations of its more remote states into a significant aspect of its present choice" (Barnes, *An Existential Ethics*, 17).

4. Barnes, *An Existential Ethics*, 16–17.

5. Barnes, *An Existential Ethics*, part 1, chapter 1.

6. We can also go a step further to distinguish between a pre-ethical choice and a non-ethical choice. A pre-ethical choice is a choice a person makes at a stage when she hasn't learned how to justify her behavior. At this pre-ethical stage she could not oppose any ethics, because she neither has nor knows any ethics. Thus, her choice is not exactly a non-ethical choice if we take "non" in the ordinary sense of negating. Now, since the valuing of the immediate self-realization can also be the result of a pre-ethical choice, here we have some additional evidence for the claim that the choice to value the immediate self-realization is not necessarily a non-ethical choice.

7. The detailed comparison of Sartre's and Kierkegaard's ethics belongs to another work.

8. "For it is the very contingency of our appearing in the world that we have to consider as an accident. . . . An accident because my project illuminates it and gives it value as what has allowed this project. We have to love having been able not to be; being *de trop*, etc. Only in this way can the *new* come into the world" (NE, 492–93).

9. "[T]he myth of God was tranquilizing. . . . My look looks within God's look, I never see anything more than the *already seen*. In this way, I am, on the one hand, tranquilized, but, on the other hand, I fall into the inessential. . . . But if God disappears, the *things seen* disappear with him (I am not yet taking up what is seen by the Other). Being remains" (NE, 494).

10. I am indebted to James Rose for his stimulating and insightful discussions on this topic.

11. E.g., see Anderson, *Sartre's Two Ethics*, 6–7.

12. According to Sartre, in authenticity we can always extend the willing of our freedom and our unreflective project to the willing of others' freedom and project. "But if I have comprehended what a man is and brought about my conversion, I do not just wish that my project should be realized, I wish that it be so by way of this man, that is, through contingency and fragility" (NE, 506).

13. Although Sartre did not have a developed theory of authenticity in *The Transcendence of the Ego*, the depreciation of the Ego (the empirical self) is one major theme there.

Chapter Eight

Conclusion: The Relation between Sartre's Ontology and Ethics

Introduction

Having discussed Sartre's ontology and ethics in detail, we are ready to draw a few conclusions concerning the relation between Sartre's ontology and ethics. In what follows, I will examine in turn the relation between freedom and absolute responsibility, the relation between bad faith and authenticity, and the relation between pure reflection and authenticity. I argue that, although we can derive the ethical features of pure reflection and bad faith from the ontological characteristics of pure reflection, we simply cannot derive the theory of authenticity or the theory of absolute responsibility from Sartre's ontology.

Freedom and Absolute Responsibility

In the chapter on freedom in *Being and Nothingness*, Sartre claimed that absolute responsibility is "simply the logical requirement of the consequences of our freedom" (EN, 695; BN, 708). According to him,

> The essential consequences of our earlier remarks [on freedom] is that man being condemned to be free carries the weight of the whole world on his shoulders; he is responsible for the world and for himself as a way of being. We are taking the word "responsibility" in its ordinary sense as "consciousness (of) being the incontestable author of an event or of an object." In this sense the responsibility of the for-itself is overwhelming since he is the one by whom it happens that *there is* a world; since he is also the one who makes himself be, then whatever may be the situation in which he finds himself, the for-itself must wholly assume this situation

137

with its peculiar coefficient of adversity, even though it be insupportable. (EN, 693; BN, 707)

At the outset Sartre's reasoning seems to be correct, for if I am free in the sense of being the non-positional "feel" that I am autonomous to form and commit myself to act on a genuine project (as we discussed in chapter 3), it does seem to follow that I am responsible for choosing the project and for the results of the project, with 'responsibility' understood in the ordinary sense that Sartre proposed above (i.e., "consciousness [of] being the incontestable author of an event [choosing the project] or of an object [the result of the project chosen]"). However, if we look closely at the reasoning, we find the fallacy of equivocation.

The above reasoning assumes that "I" am the "incontestable author of an event or of an object." This assumption is acceptable only if we take "I" in the sense of an empirical agent, for (1) an author in the ordinary sense is an empirical agent, and (2) responsibility in the ordinary sense is responsibility *of an agent*. However, when the word 'I' appears in the description of the non-positional "feel" (of) freedom, it does not refer to an empirical agent; rather, it refers to the non-personal, on-going "feel." Thus, there is an implicit equivocation of the word 'I' in the above reasoning. Therefore, the reasoning is not correct.

Not only is freedom in Sartre's technical sense not a sufficient condition for absolute responsibility, but also, it is not a necessary condition for absolute responsibility. It is not hard to imagine a case in which we have absolute responsibility and yet we are not free in Sartre's technical sense. For example, suppose we are omniscient and omnipotent. In that case, we are absolutely responsible for everything we do, and yet we are not free in Sartre's technical sense.

In general, a problem exists in Sartre's including "responsibility" in his system as a legitimate notion. Responsibility is always a responsibility of *someone*. But in Sartre's system we cannot find a plausible candidate for this *someone*. She cannot be the empirical self, because the empirical self is merely an object for consciousness, not an ontological being. Can she then be the self we proposed in the last chapter? No. If she is the self in the first sense—the present non-positional consciousness—how can we make sense of the claim that the present non-positional consciousness is absolutely responsible for anything that is brought forth by the past non-positional consciousness? If she is the self in the second sense—the common part of all non-positional consciousness—we have this problem. The common part of all non-positional consciousness cannot have any effect or bring forth anything in the world (since the common part is intended-intending). Given that, how can we make sense of the claim that the common part of all non-positional consciousness is absolutely responsible for anything that is brought forth by the past non-positional consciousness, which we know is not brought forth by the common part of all non-positional consciousness?

Bad Faith and Authenticity

Bad faith does not exhaust the category of inauthenticity. Bad faith is certainly an inauthentic behavior, but a common unreflective project of becoming God (e.g., to be a salesman), which does not have to be in bad faith, also falls under the category of inauthenticity (NE, 559).

In chapter 4, I argued that the ontological characteristics of bad faith do not have salient and non-trivial ethical implications. We have seen that we cannot satisfactorily explain why bad faith is bad in the ethical sense, on the basis of the ontological structure of bad faith. If so, in what sense is bad faith bad?

Bad faith is bad because it gets in the way of authenticity and pure reflection. As I said in the previous chapter, bad faith and authenticity are mutually exclusive.[1] If we are in bad faith, we are not authentic. If we are authentic, we are not in bad faith. There is no way to be authentically in bad faith. To be authentically in bad faith is no longer in bad faith; it is a form of cynicism.[2]

It might be objected that this explanation of the badness of bad faith does not really tell us anything because it is question begging. Of course it is question begging. It is no easier to explain why authenticity and pure reflection are ethically good. However, this explanation is not totally uninformative. It at least shows that the ethical character of bad faith derives from somewhere else, possibly from the ontological characteristics of pure reflection and authenticity.

Pure Reflection and Authenticity

In chapter 5, I argued that pure reflection yields knowledge that has normative universality. However, it does not seem obvious that this normativity can readily be linked to Sartre's ethics. For this normativity is *not* an ethical normativity. It does not provide norms for our actions. It is rather a normativity that accounts for the "ought" in our self-knowledge. If so, does it mean that the ontological characteristics of pure reflection do not have ethical implications? Let's consider it carefully.

At first sight, there seems to be an easy way to link Sartre's ontology with the ethical significance of pure reflection. Suppose Sartre's ontology is correct, that is, the ontological descriptions in *Being and Nothingness* are true. We know from common sense that we value truth. And because we value truth, we also value the procedure that can produce truth. Now, because the ontological descriptions in *Being and Nothingness*—including those descriptions of pure reflection—are true, pure reflection is indeed the procedure through which all ontological descriptions are made. Hence, we value pure reflection insofar as (1) we value the ontological descriptions and (2) pure reflection is the procedure that produces the ontological descriptions. Because we value pure reflection, we have the ground to claim that pure reflection is ethically significant.

Unfortunately, this argument does not work, for there are two serious objections to the argument.

First, one might object that the above argument has an implausible consequence: If the argument works, it follows that *any* ontological theory that discusses the methodological procedure that brings forth the ontological descriptions in question has the implication that the methodological procedure is ethically significant. Note that in the argument above it is not the case that *what the ontological descriptions say* suggests pure reflection has value. It is rather through our valuing the truth of the ontological descriptions that we value pure reflection. The language in which the ontological descriptions are given is the object language. The language in which we talk about and value the truth of the ontological descriptions is the metalanguage. When we argue that ontological descriptions implies our valuing pure reflection in the above argument, we are not arguing for an implication in the object language; rather, we are arguing for an implication in the metalanguage. To put it more precisely, we may say the following: Let p be the conjunction of the ontological descriptions in the object language. Let q be the name of p in the metalanguage. Let r be the claim that pure reflection has value. What we really argued for in the above argument is the thesis that q's being true implies r (call it "thesis 1"), rather than the thesis that p implies r (call it "thesis 2"), the thesis we should have argued for. Note that thesis 1 and thesis 2 are different. In the context of the above argument, thesis 1 has the implication that any ontological descriptions—as long as it discusses pure reflection as a methodological procedure that produces the ontological descriptions—imply that pure reflection has value, whereas thesis 2 does not.

Second, one might argue that it is our knowing the ontological descriptions being true rather than the ontological descriptions' being true that makes us value pure reflection. And yet in the argument above, our supposition is that the ontological descriptions are true, not that we know the ontological descriptions are true.

Having shown that the above way of linking Sartre's ontology with the ethical significance of pure reflection does not work, let me argue that the ethical significance of pure reflection does follow from Sartre's ontology. Suppose Sartre's ontology is correct. Then the ontological descriptions of pure reflection are true. So pure reflection does produce knowledge that has normative universality. Now, it is manifest from the very notion of normative universality that purely reflective knowledge serves as a norm for knowledge. Because nothing can be a norm without our valuing it, we value the purely reflectively knowledge. Accordingly, insofar as it is through pure reflection that we obtain purely reflective knowledge, we value pure reflection, and hence we have ground to claim the ethical significance of pure reflection. In sum, the ontological characteristics of pure reflection do imply the ethical significance of pure reflection in the way we just sketched.

Morever, if we understand the "badness" of bad faith as its hindrance to pure reflection, the ontological characteristics of pure reflection can account for the ethical feature of bad faith, insofar as they account for the ethical significance of pure reflection.

Although the ontological characteristics of pure reflection support the ethical features of pure reflection and bad faith, they do not really support the ethical features of authenticity (pure reflection*). We know pure reflection is not exactly authenticity, for impure reflection does not exhaust inauthenticity.[3] Authenticity presupposes and contains pure reflection, but it is pure reflection plus something more—the three ethical features we discussed in the previous chapter. Underlying the three ethical features of authenticity is ultimately the passion for the revival of the childish heart. And yet there is nothing in the ontological structure of pure reflection or in any other part of Sartre's ontology that can support or account for the passion for the revival of the childish heart. Therefore, although some parts of Sartre's ethics (the ethical features of bad faith and pure reflection) follow from his ontology, Sartre's theory of authenticity cannot be founded on his ontology.

Conclusion

To sum up, there are more connections between Sartre's ontology and ethics than most people realize. The ontological characteristics of pure reflection do imply the ethical features of pure reflection and bad faith. Nevertheless, on the whole, Sartre's ethics cannot founded on his ontology. His theory of absolute responsibility does not follow from his theory of freedom. And his theory of authenticity does not follow from the ontology he developed in *Being and Nothingness*. In spite of Sartre's claim that his ethics follows from his ontology in *Being and Nothingness*, and his effort to develop an ethics on the basis of his ontology in *Notebooks for an Ethics*, there are gaps between Sartre's ontology and ethics that cannot be filled in.

Notes

1.   So is bad faith and pure reflection.
2.   Similar things can be said with respect to the relation between bad faith and pure reflection.
3.   Although impure reflection exhausts the realm of inauthentic reflective behavior, it does not cover the realm of inauthentic unreflective behavior, i.e., the realm of the unreflective project of trying to be God.

Selected Bibliography

Anderson, Thomas. "Neglected Sartrean Arguments for the Freedom of Consciousness." *Philosophy Today* 17 (1973): 28–38.

———. "Freedom as Supreme Value: The Ethics of Sartre and de Beauvoir." *Proceedings of the Catholic Philosophical Association* 50 (1976): 60–71.

———. *The Foundation and Structure of Sartrean Ethics.* Lawrence, Kans.: The Regents Press of Kansas, 1979.

———. "Sartre's Early Ethics and the Ontology of *Being and Nothingness.*" In *Sartre Alive*, edited by Ronald Aronson. Detroit: Wayne State University Press, 1991.

———. *Authenticity, Conversion, and the City of Ends in Sartre's Notebooks for an Ethics* in *Writing the Politics of Difference.* Albany, N.Y.: SUNY Press, 1991.

———. *Sartre's Two Ethics: From Authenticity to Integral Humanity.* Chicago: Open Court, 1993.

Aronson, Ronald, ed. *Sartre Alive.* Detroit: Wayne State University Press, 1991.

Barnes, Hazel. *An Existentialist Ethics.* New York: Alfred A. Knopf, 1967.

———. "Sartre on the Emotions." *Journal of the British Society of Phenomenology* 15 (1984): 3–15.

———. "Sartre's Ontology." In *The Cambridge Companion to Sartre,* edited by Christina Howells. New York: Cambridge University Press, 1992.

Beauvoir, Simone de. *The Ethics of Ambiguity,* translated by Bernard Frechtman. New York: Citadel Press, 1964.

143

Bell, Linda. *Sartre's Ethics of Authenticity*. Tuscaloosa, Ala.: University of Alabama Press, 1989.

Bergmann, Frithjof. "Sartre on the Nature of Consciousness." *American Philosophical Quarterly* 19 (1982): 153–62.

Bergoffen, Debra. "Sartre's Transcendence of the Ego: A Methodological Reading." *Philosophy Today* 22 (1978): 244–51.

———. "The Look as Bad Faith." *Philosophy Today* 36 (1992): 221–27.

Blosser, Philip. "The Status of Mental Images in Sartre's Theory of Consciousness." *Southern Journal of Philosophy* 24 (1986): 163–72.

Busch, Thomas. "Sartre: The Phenomenological Reduction and Human Relationships." *Journal of the British Society for Phenomenology* 6 (1975): 55–61.

———. "Sartre's Use of the Reduction: *Being and Nothingness* Reconsidered." In *Jean-Paul Sartre: Contemporary Approaches to his Philosophy*. Ed. H. Silverman and F. Elliston. Pittsburgh: Duquesne University Press, 1980.

———. *The Power of Consciousness and the Force of Circumstances in Sartre's Philosophy*. Bloomington: Indiana University Press, 1990.

———. "Sartre on Surpassing the Given." *Philosophy Today* 35 (1991): 26–31.

Carnap, Rudolf. "Empiricism, Semantics, and Ontology." In *Semantics and the Philosophy of Language*. Ed. L. Linsky. Urbana: University of Illinois Press, 1952.

———. *Meaning and Necessity*. Chicago: University of Chicago Press, 1960.

Catalano, Joseph. *A Commentary on Jean-Paul Sartre's Being and Nothingness*. New York: Harper & Row, 1974.

———. "On the Possibility of Good Faith." *Man and World* 13 (1980): 207–28.

———. "Good and Bad Faith: Weak and Strong Notions." *Review of the Existential Psychological Psychiat* 17 (1980-81): 79–90.

———. "Successfully Lying to Oneself: A Sartrean Perspective." *Philosophy and Phenomenological Research* 50 (1990): 673–93.

———. "Authenticity: A Sartrean Perspective." *Philosophy Forum* (1990-1991): 99–119.

———. "Reinventing the Transcendental Ego." *Man and World* 28 (1995): 101–11.

———. *Good Faith and Other Essays: Perspectives on a Sartrean Ethics*. Lanham, Md.: Rowman & Littlefield, 1996.

Caws, Peter. *Sartre*. London: Routledge & Kegan Paul, 1979.

Chisholm, Roderick, ed. *Realism and the Background of Phenomenology*. Glencoe, Ill.: Free Press, 1960.

Compton, John. "Sartre, Merleau-Ponty, and Human Freedom." *Journal of Philosophy* 19 (1982): 577–88.

Coueslant, Monica. "The Nature of Sartre's Ethics: A Reconciliation of its Ideal and Positive Elements." *Man and World* 22 (1989): 151–61.

Cumming, Robert. "Role-playing: Sartre's Transformation of Husserl's Phenomenology." In *The Cambridge Companion to Sartre*. Ed. C. Howell. Cambridge: Cambridge University Press, 1992.

Danto, Arthur. *Jean-Paul Sartre*. New York: The Viking Press, 1975.

Detmer, David. *Freedom as a Value: A Critique of the Ethical Theory of Jean-Paul Sartre*. La Salle, Ill.: Open Court, 1988.

Dinan, Stephen. "Intentionality in the Introduction to *Being and Nothingness*." *Research in Phenomenology* 1 (1971): 91–118.

———. "Spontaneity and Perception in Sartre's Theory of the Body." *Philosophy Today* 23 (1979): 279–91.

Fell, Joseph. *Emotions in the Thought of Sartre*. New York: Columbia University Press, 1965.

Føllesdal, Dagfinn. "Sartre on Freedom." In *The Philosophy of Jean-Paul Sartre*. Ed. P. Schilpp. La Salle, Illinois: Open Court, 1981.

Frondizi, Risieri. "Sartre's Early Ethics: A Critique." In *The Philosophy of Jean-Paul Sartre*. Ed. P. Schilpp. La Salle, Illinois: Open Court, 1981.

Glynn, Simon, ed. *Sartre: An Investigation of Some Major Themes*. Gower, 1987.

Gordon, Jeffrey. "Bad Faith: A Dilemma." *Philosophy* 60 (1985): 258–62.

Grossmann, Reinhardt. *Phenomenology and Existentialism*. London: Routeledge and Kegan Paul, 1984.

Gunter, P. A. Y. "Bergson and Sartre: The Rise of French Existentialism." In *The Crisis in Modernism*. Ed. F. Burwick. Cambridge: Cambridge University Press, 1992.

Hacker, P. M. S. "Davidson on the Ontology and Logical Form of Belief." *Philosophy* 73 (1998): 81–96.

Hall, Ronald. *"Freedom: Merleau-Ponty's Critique of Sartre." Philosophy Research Archive* 6 (1980): no. 1391.

Hartmann, Klaus. *Sartre's Ontology: A Study of Being and Nothingness in the Light of Hegel's Logic*. Evanston, Illinois: Northwestern University Press, 1966.

Haynes-Curtis, Carole. "The 'Faith' of Bad Faith." *Philosophy* 63 (1988): 269–75.

Hendley, Steven. *Reason and Relativism: A Sartrean Investigations.* Lexington Books, 1991.

Hegel, G. W. F. *The Phenomenology of Mind.* Trans. J. Baillie. New York: Humanities Press, 1977.

Heidegger, Martin. *Being and Time.* Trans. J. Macquarrie and E. Robinson. New York: Harper & Row, 1962.

———. *Basic Writings.* Ed. D. Krell. New York: Harper & Row, 1977.

Holmes, Richard. "Being-in-itself Revisited." *Dialogue* 23 (1984): 397–406.

Howells, Christina. *Sartre: The Necessity of Freedom.* Cambridge: Cambridge University Press, 1988.

———. *The Cambridge Companion to Sartre.* Cambridge: Cambridge University Press, 1992.

Husserl, Edmund. *Cartesian Meditations.* Trans. D. Cairns. Boston: Martinus Nijhoff, 1960.

———. *Formal and Transcendental Logic.* Trans. D. Cairns. The Hague: Martinus Nijhoff, 1969.

———. *Idea II.* In *Collected Works*, vol. 2. The Hague: Martinus Nijhoff, 1980.

———. *The Idea of Phenomenology.* Trans. W. Alston and G. Nakhnikian. The Hague: Martinus Nijhoff, 1950.

———. *Ideas: General Introduction to Pure Phenomenology.* Trans. W. Gibson. New York: Macmillan, 1931.

———. *Logical Investigations* 2 vols. Trans. J. Findlay. New York: Humanities Press, 1970.

———. *On the Phenomenology of the Consciousness of Internal Time.* Trans. by J. Barnett Brough. Boston: Kluwer Academic Publishers, 1991.

———. "Phenomenology." (For the *Encyclopaedia Britannica*.) In *Husserl, Shorter Works*. Ed. P. McCormick and F. Elliston. Notre Dame: University of Notre Dame Press, 1981.

———. *Studies in the Phenomenology of Constitution.* Trans. R. Rojcewicz and A. Schuwer. Boston: Kluwer Academic Publishers, 1989.

Hymers, Michael. "Bad Faith." *Philosophy* 64 (1989): 397–402.

Irwin, William. "Sartre on the Emotions: A New Evaluation." *Dialogue* (PST) 38, no.1 (1995): 1–7.

Jeanson, Francis. *Sartre and the Problem of Morality.* Trans. R. Stone. Bloomington: Indiana University Press, 1980.

Kant, Immanuel. *Critique of Pure Reason.* Trans. N. Smith. London: Macmillan, 1929.

Kaufmann, Walter. *Without Guilt and Justice.* New York: Delta, 1973.

Khan, R. F. "D. Z. Phillips on Waiters and Bad Faith." *Philosophy* 59 (1984): 389–91.

Kenevan, Phyllis. "Self-consciousness and the Ego in the Philosophy of Sartre." In *The Philosophy of Jean-Paul Sartre.* Ed. P. Schilpp. La Salle, Illinois: Open Court, 1981.

Kierkegaard, Søren. *Kierkegaard's Writings.* Princeton: Princeton University Press, 1980.

Langer, Monika. "Sartre and Mealeau-Ponty: A Reappraisal." In *The Philosophy of Jean-Paul Sartre.* Ed. P. Schilpp. La Salle, Chicago: Open Court, 1981.

Levinas, Emmanuel. *La Theorie de l'intuition dans la phenomenologie de Husserl.* Paris: Felix Alcan, 1930.

———. *The Theory of Intuition in Husserl's Phenomenology.* Trans. A. Orianne. Evanston, Ill.: Northwestern University Press, 1973.

Manser, Anthony. "Unfair to Waiters?" *Philosophy* 58 (1983): 102–6.

———. "A New Look at Bad Faith." In *Sartre: An Investigation of Some Major Themes.* Ed. S. Glynn. Gower, 1987.

———. "The Non-being of Nothingness." *Journal of British Society of Phenomenology* 19 (1988): 90–92.

———. "Sartre on Temporality." *Journal of British Society of Phenomenology* 20 (1989): 23-32.

Marcuse, Hubert. "Sartre's Existentialism." In *Studies in Critical Philosophy.* Boston: Beacon Press, 1973.

Mark, James. "The Waiter and the Philosopher." *Philosophy* 58 (1983): 386–88.

Martin, Michael. "Sartre on Lying to Oneself," *Philosophy Research Archive* 4 (1978): no. 1252.

McCulloch, Gregory. *Using Sartre: An Analytical Introduction to Early Sartrean Themes.* London: Routledge and Kegan Paul, 1994.

McInerney, Peter. "Sartre on Self-determination." *Journal of Philosophy* 76 (1979): 663–77.

Mensch, James. "Husserl and Sartre: A Question of Reason." *Journal of Philosophical Research* 19 (1994): 147–84.

Merleau-Ponty, Maurice. *Phenomenology of Perception.* Trans. C. Smith.

London: Routledge and Kegan Paul, 1989.

Mirvish, Adrian. "Gestalt Mechanisms and Believing Beliefs: Sartre's Analysis of the Phenomenon of Bad Faith." *Journal of British Society of Phenomenology* 18 (1987): 245–62.

———. "Sartre on Embodied Minds, Authenticity and Childhood." *Man and World* 29, no. 1 (1996): 19–41.

Moreland, John. "For-itself and In-itself in Sartre and Merleau-Ponty." *Philosophy Today* 17 (1973): 311–18.

Morris, Phyllis. "Self-deception: Sartre's Resolution of the Paradox." In *Jean-Paul Sartre.* Ed. H. Silverman. Pittsburgh: Duquesne University Press, 1980.

———. "Sartre on the Transcendence of the Ego." *Philosophy and Phenomenological Research* 46 (1985): 179–98.

———. "Sartre on the Self-Deceiver's Translucent Consciousness." *Journal of British Society of Phenomenology* 23 (1992): 103–19.

Neu, Jerome. "Divided Minds: Sartre's 'Bad Faith' Critique of Freud." *Review of Metaphysics* 42 (1988): 79–101.

Phillips, D. Z. "Bad Faith and Sartre's Waiter." *Philosophy* 56 (1981): 23–32.

Quine, W. V. *Word and Object.* Technology Press of MIT, 1960.

Rosenberg, Jay. "Apperception and Sartre's 'Pre-reflective *Cogito*'." *American Philosophical Quarterly* 18 (1981): 255–60.

Ross, Howard. "Merleau-Ponty and Jean-Paul Sartre on the Nature of Consciousness." *Cogito* 3 (1985): 115–21.

Russell, Michael. "Reflection and Self-deception." *Research in Phenomenology* 11 (1981): 62–74.

Santoni, Ronald. "Sartre on 'Sincerity': 'Bad Faith'? Or Equivocation?" *Personalist* 53 (1972): 150–60.

———. "Bad Faith and 'Lying to Oneself'." *Philosophy and Phenomenological Research* 38 (1978): 384–98.

———. "Sartre on Sincerity — A Reconsideration." *Philosophy Today* 29 (1985): 142–47.

———. "Morality, Authenticity and God." *Philosophy Today* 31 (1987): 242–52.

———. "The Cynicism of Sartre's 'Bad Faith'." *International Philosophical Quarterly* 30 (1990): 3–15.

———. *Bad Faith, Good Faith, and Authenticity in Sartre's Early Philosophy.* Philadelphia: Temple University Press, 1995.

Sartre, Jean-Paul. *Anti-Semite and Jew.* Trans. G. Becker. New York:

Schocken, 1974.

——. *Being and Nothingness: A Phenomenological Essay on Ontology*. Trans. Hazel Barnes. Pocket Books, 1992.

——. *Cahiers pour une morale*. Ed. A. Elkaïm-Sartre. Paris: NRF, Gallimard, 1983.

——. "Consciousness of Self and Knowledge of Self." In *Readings in Existential Phenomenology*. Ed. N. Lawrence and D. O'Connor. Prentice-Hall, 1967.

——. *Critique of Dialectical Reason*, vols. 1 and 2. Trans. Q. Hoare. New York: Verso, 1991.

——. *The Emotions: Outline of A Theory*. Trans. B. Frechtman. New York: The Philosophical Library, 1948.

——. *Esquisse d'une théirie des émotions*. Paris: Hermann, 1965.

——. *Existentialism*. Trans. B. Frechtman. New York: The Philosophical Library, 1947.

——. "Existentialism is a Humanism." In *Existentialism from Dostoevsky to Sartre*. Ed. W. Kaufmann. New York: New American Library, 1989.

——. *L'existentialisme est un humanisme*. Paris: Nagel, 1946.

——. *L'etre et le neant*. Paris: Gallimard, 1943.

——. "Une Ideé foundamentale de la phénoménologie de Husserl: L'Intentionalité." *La Nouvelle Revue francaise*, no. 304 (1939): 129–31.

——. *L'Imagination*. Paris: Librairie Felix Alcan, 1936.

——. *Imagination: A Psychological Critique*. Trans. F. William. Ann Arbor: University of Michigan Press, 1962.

——. *L'Imaginaire: Psychologie phénoménologique de l'imagination*. Paris: NRF, Gallimard, 1948.

——. "Intentionality: A Fundamental Idea of Husserl's Phenomenology." Trans. J. Fell. *The Journal of the British Society for Phenomenology* 1 (1970): 4–5.

——. *Nausea*. Trans. R. Baldick. Penguin Books, 1965.

——. *No Exit and Three Other Plays*. Trans. S. Gilbert and L. Abel. New York: Vintage, 1955.

——. *Notebooks for an Ethics*. Trans. D. Pellauer. Chicago: University of Chicago Press, 1992.

——. *The Psychology of Imagination*. New York: Citadel Press, 1963.

——. *Sartre on Theater*. Ed. M. Contat and M. Rybalka. Trans. F. Jellinek. New York: Pantheon Books, 1976.

——. *Search for a Method*. Trans. H. Barnes. New York: Alfred A.

Knopf, 1963.

———. *La Transendence de l'Ego*. Paris: J. Vrin, 1966.

———. *The Transcendence of the Ego*. Trans. F. William and R. Kirkpatrick. New York: Farrar, Strauss, and Giroux, 1988.

———. *Truth and Existence*. Trans. A. den Hoven. Chicago: University of Chicago Press, 1992.

———. *The War Diaries of Jean-Paul Sartre*. Trans. Q. Hoare. New York: Pantheon Books, 1985.

Schilpp, Paul. *The Philosophy of Jean-Paul Sartre*. La Salle, Ill.: Open Court, 1981.

Sheridan, James. *Sartre: the Radical Conversion*. Ohio: Ohio University Press, 1969.

Silverman, Hugh, et al., eds. *Jean-Paul Sartre: Contemporary Approaches to His Philosophy*. Pittburgh: Duquesne University Press, 1980.

Smoot, William. "The Concept of Authenticity in Sartre." *Man and World* 7 (1974): 135–48.

Spade, Paul. *Jean-Paul Sartre's Being and Nothingness: Class Notes*.1995.

Stevenson, Leslie. "Sartre on Bad Faith." *Philosophy* 58 (1983): 253–58.

Steward, Jon. "Merleau-Ponty's Criticisms of Sartre's Theory of Freedom." *Philosophy Today* 39 (1995): 311–24.

Vaughan, Christopher. *Pure Reflection, Self-knowledge, and Moral Understanding in the Philosophy of Jean-Paul Sartre*. (Dissertation.) Bloomington: Indiana University, 1993.

Walker, A. D. M. "Sartre, Santoni, and Sincerity." *Personalist* 58 (1977): 88–92.

Warnock, Mary. *Existentialist Ethics*. New York: St. Martin's Press, 1967.

———. *The Philosophy of Jean-Paul Sartre*. New York: Barnes & Noble, 1967.

Weberman, David. "Sartre on Emotions, and Wallowing." *American Philosophical Quarterly* 33 (1996): 393–407.

Whitford, Magaret. *Merleau Ponty's Critique of Sartre's Philosophy*. Lexington French Forum, 1982.

Whitney, Peter. "Sartre's Phenomenological Description of Bad Faith: Intentionality as Ontological Ground of Existence." *Philosophy Today* 24 (1980): 238–48.

Wider, Kathleen. "Through the Looking Glass: Sartre on Knowledge and the Preflective '*Cogito*'." *Man and World* 22 (1989): 329–43.

———. "Sartre and the Long Distance Truth Driver: The Reflexivity of Consciousness." *Journal of British Society of Phenomenology* 24

(1993): 232-49.

————. "The Failure of Self-consciousness in Sartre's *Being and Nothingness.*" *Dialogue* 32 (1993): 737–56.

————. *The Bodily Nature of Consciousness.* Ithaca: Cornell University Press, 1997.

Wilcocks, Robert, ed. *Critical Essays on Jean-Paul Sartre.* Boston, Massachusetts: G. K. Hall & Co., 1988.

Wild, John. "Authentic Existence." *Ethics* 75 (1965): 227–35.

Zheng, Yiwei. "Ontology and Ethics in Sartre's *Being and Nothingness*: On the Condition of the Possibility of Bad Faith." *Southern Journal of Philosophy* 35 (1997): 265–87.

————. "On Sartre's 'Non-Positional Consciousness'." *Southwest Philosophy Review* 16, no. 1 (2000): 141–49.

————. "On Pure Reflection in Sartre's *Being and Nothingness.*" *Sartre Studies International* 7, no. 1 (2001): 19–42.

————. "On Freedom in Sartre's *Being and Nothingness.*" *Southwest Philosophy Review* 18, no. 1 (2002): 173–84.

————. "Sartre on Authenticity," *Sartre Studies International* 8, no. 2 (2002): 127–40.

Index